I Owe It All to Rock & Roll (and the CBC)

a memoir

Frank Cameron

With a Foreword by Bobby Curtola

Pottersfield Press, Lawrencetown Beach, Nova Scotia, Canada

Library and Archives Canada Cataloguing in Publication

Cameron, Frank, 1938-, author
I owe it all to rock & roll (and the CBC) / Frank Cameron.
ISBN 978-1-897426-65-4
1. Cameron, Frank, 1938-. 2. Radio broadcasters--Nova Scotia--Biography. I. Title.
ML429.C182I64 2015 384.54092 C2014-907310-0

Cover design by Gail LeBlanc
Cover image: Frank Cameron's personal collection

We acknowledge the financial support of the Government of Canada through the Canada Book Fund for our publishing activities. We acknowledge the support of the Canada Council for the Arts, which last year invested $157 million to bring the arts to Canadians throughout the country. Nous remercions le Conseil des arts du Canada de son soutien. L'an dernier, le Conseil a investi 157 millions de dollars pour mettre de l'art dans la vie des Canadiennes et des Canadiens de tout le pays. Pottersfield Press recognizes the support of the Province of Nova Scotia through Film and Creative Industries Nova Scotia. We are pleased to work in partnership with the agency to develop and promote our creative industries for the benefit of all Nova Scotians.

Pottersfield Press
83 Leslie Road
East Lawrencetown, Nova Scotia, Canada, B2Z 1P8
Website: www.PottersfieldPress.com
To order, phone 1-800-NIMBUS9 (1-800-646-2879) www.nimbus.ns.ca

Canada The Canada Council for the Arts Le Conseil des Arts du Canada FILM & CREATIVE INDUSTRIES NOVA SCOTIA

Dedication

This book is dedicated to my father, Harvey Gilmour Cameron, who died in 1960 at age fifty-three. My dad was a very quiet man, but he taught me more about life than anyone. Someone once asked me who I thought was the smartest man in the world. The expected answer was Jesus Christ, but I said, "My father." His knowledge of history and his grasp of the English language were unsurpassed. I remember writing an essay in high school where I used the phrase "ages ago." My father suggested "aeons and aeons." Dad was older and wiser than me, and I respected his use of the language. I wrote this book for you, Dad. I know that you're proud of your only son.

Acknowledgements

I would like to thank Chris, who is my rock, and my children and grandchildren, who taught me how to give and receive unconditional love.

Contents

Foreword by Bobby Curtola 7

1 Beginnings, Humble and Otherwise 11

2 New Glasgow and CKEC Radio 28

3 Truro, a Town Without Strong Drink 43

4 The Weird and the Wonderful: CHNS 54

5 1964: Of Frank's Bandstand, Beatles, and Other Happenings 65

6 CBC: A Cast of Characters 74

7 Of Pranks and Professionals 92

8 England, Trudeau, and Politics (sort of) 106

9 In Which I Rub Elbows With Some Famous People 113

10 Retirement, Scotland, and Seaside 121

Foreword
by Bobby Curtola

It is with great pleasure that I write this foreword for my dear friend, Frank Cameron. This book is a magical story about radio and how important it was to our generation of the 1950s and '60s.

Of course, Frank's career spans a much greater time period, which he covers here, but when you understand what he was able to achieve in those early years, you will understand how he moved through his career and became a media personality, the voice of his generation, respected by all his peers. Frank was at the top in the '60s, the number one radio personality in the Maritimes, who understood the art of his business.

Most people today don't realize the pioneering role Frank played in those early years. He was one of a handful of DJs across Canada who had direct access to all teens in their individual markets through their radio shows. He was a huge celebrity. Over the years, teenagers would phone in to his shows, chat, request their favourite songs and talk about their life. He literally introduced people like me to his fans. Most of us early recording artists had no other way to reach our audience except through radio or the press, and radio was the best way. Everything in an artist's career changed if a station like CHNS or a guy like Frank Cameron played your record.

Before there was what we today call "interactive," Frank was talking to his fans, asking them what they liked, playing their requests and dedications. He knew what they wanted to hear and played it. Those were the days of what the music industry called "Personality Radio," where the DJ, not a computer as we have today, picked the songs and programmed his show. Frank had his ear to the ground and knew what we wanted to hear on radio. He was the most popular DJ in the Maritimes for years and no one has beaten his record or achievements since. A lot of great personalities followed, but Frank was the first and the biggest star.

When his shows expanded to television as the Maritime host for *Music Hop*, the cross-Canada variety show on CBC, he launched even more artists' recording careers and became a national celebrity. Frank always played the hits first, before everyone else.

His story is mixed with humour because Frank always loves to make you laugh. As you go on this journey with Frank, those great times of your youth will come back to you. Those moments that changed you, the path you chose – Frank was there. He was the thread of our youth and our growth. When the transistor radio was born, we could take our music, and Frank, with us. Those were the days of the Coca-Cola Hi-Fi Club, the Top Ten, the CHNS Hits Chart with Frank's picks.

Can you remember those numerous dance halls and high school dances? How about those shows and concerts at the arena? The weekends were ours! We were alive with our music and in the moment. When you look back, you realize that the songs connected us. It was a time when we all got to dream, and a time when we all began to create our beautiful life's journey. It truly was our *Happy Days*.

Frank was there, the beacon who talked us through it all, and for that, as an artist and friend, I am very grateful to him. My perspective was a little different from the stage, but I was a teen then too and, just like all the rest of us, enjoying every moment.

God bless you, Frank, and congratulations for achieving another milestone in your life. This is a wonderful story of a time in music where borders didn't exist, just the music the world called rock and roll. You were, and are, a part of an exclusive club of radio personalities in Canada who were the voice of our generation, and we thank you for being a major part of our life's story.

1

Beginnings, Humble and Otherwise

It was early September, 1964. I rushed down the basement hall of the CBC building on Bell Road in Halifax, Nova Scotia. It was the fourth time in an hour that I had deposited myself on the porcelain bowl.

I was about to appear on television for the first time. I nervously stared at the unimaginative graffiti while I contemplated a few questions. What if I bomb? I'm about to host a TV show for teenagers. Am I too old? I'm twenty-six, for heaven's sake. What is the meaning of life? And the most important question of all. How did I get here? That one I can answer, but it could take a while. Bear with me.

It all started in 1773 when the good ship *Hector* arrived in Loch Broom near Pictou, Nova Scotia. Scots were a disposable commodity in Scotland, where more sheep needed more room to graze. A sturdy young Scot named Alexander Cameron waded ashore and finally settled in the Pictou area. The Mi'kmaw were already there. If it were not for them, Alexander and his friends wouldn't have made it through the first winter. Their story is chronicled at the *Hector* quay in Pictou.

Alexander was one of two Camerons in the scurvy-ridden bunch, and before long he was begatting little Camerons. This is where I came in. I was born in 1938 in the old Aberdeen Hospital in New Glasgow, Nova Scotia, not far from the place where Alexander had landed 165 years earlier. I gave my mother a rough time. I weighed almost eleven pounds.

My childhood was great. We moved around New Glasgow a lot. My one small problem was that every time we moved, my parents neglected to tell me where the new house was. My sister Beverly, for a small fee, would give me that information.

At the tender age of three, I spread my wings and decided I was going to the post office. I didn't know where the hell it was, but I grabbed my little red wagon and pulled it from the west side of New Glasgow across the bridge to the downtown area and I made it to the post office. Fortunately, the postmaster was a friend of my parents, so he knew who I was and saw to it that I returned home unscathed. That was my first time away from home and I enjoyed every minute of it.

I started school in 1944. The war was on, but I didn't pay much attention to it. I was busy speeding down Warren Street pulling that same red wagon with the wind in my hair and Dawn in the seat. Dawn went on to become a great artist and sculptor. You may know her as Dawn MacNutt.

I was a member of the West Side School Rhythm Band in 1944-45. I played the triangle. It's a little piece of metal shaped like a ... wait for it ... triangle. You had a little metal stick that miraculously made a kind of music when you struck the triangle with it. In that very same band was a guy named John Hamm, who became

The little red wagon, albeit in black and white, that carried me on my first trip from home. To the post office and beyond!

The West Side School Rhythm Band, 1944. I'm second from the left in the back row – you can tell by the rather large ears and the haircut that looks as if someone put a bowl on my head and cut around it. John Hamm is in the back row, fifth from the left.

a doctor like his father before him, and entered politics in 1993. In 1999 he led his Progressive Conservative Party to victory in a Nova Scotia election. He remained in office until he resigned in 2005 as premier and leader of the party. John Hamm was a real gentleman and a true Tory.

That's as opposed to the bunch running the country today. They're not even Conservatives, let alone Tories. Peter MacKay sold out his Progressive Conservative Party to the Reform Party from Alberta. Peter is much younger than me, but I know his father Elmer MacKay. Elmer was a Progressive Conservative, or Tory if you will. The story is told that Peter and some friends from Dalhousie Law School enjoyed evenings on the weekends at a hotel in Halifax where they might have smoked a little of the ganja. One evening while the smokers were happily ensconced in the hotel room, a posse arrived from the RCMP. Someone happened to be in the hotel lobby and overheard the RCMP ask the desk clerk in what room these future lawyers might be. He quickly called the room on the house phone and told the crew that the Mounties were on the way up and they should hide the dope. So they threw a blanket over Peter.

Like most kids, I had the usual childhood diseases, plus some additional stuff thrown in for good measure. I lost my tonsils when I was four. I never did find them.

When I was nine years old, I contracted spinal meningitis. I remember two things about that. The spinal tap and memories of it still send chills up my spine. Doctors and nurses turned my ass into a pincushion. One of those nurses was my aunt Elda, my mother's sister. They injected me with the new wonder drug penicillin. They stopped when it started to come out my ears. Even then I had enormous ears. I was known to my friends as Flaps. My father said I looked like a taxi going down the street with both doors open. My mother didn't know if I would walk or fly. Every time my cousins saw me they would break into a chorus of "Red Sails in the Sunset." Cruel.

I also had an attack of appendicitis when I was nine. Very painful, but I got to keep my appendix. I'm told the appendix is still a mystery to most medical professionals, and it's an organ we don't really need. But I still have mine if anybody needs one.

While we're on the subject of pain, I developed a kidney stone in the late '80s. A urologist told me it's like an uncut diamond going through your urinary system. It felt more like a broken Coke bottle, but I passed it. Women who have had kidney stones say they would rather have a baby any day. This same urologist asked me what liquid I drank to flush my kidneys. He gave me the top three. I'm not making this up. Number one: draught beer. It must be draught. Bottled beer has chemicals. Number two: cranberry juice. Number three: water. I think the good doctor owned a brewery.

Both my parents were great people. I have lots of good memories of my father, Harvey, who spent one of the war years in Newfoundland. He tried to sign up for overseas duty in the engineering corps, but the government wouldn't let him go. He suffered from a heart murmur. The United States Air Force came to town looking for surveyors to go to Newfoundland, which was not part of Canada then. So off he went. He helped survey the runways for Torbay Airport, now known as St. John's International. When he returned from Newfoundland he became an air raid warden. He wore a helmet and carried a flashlight. I wanted in on the deal, so I got my own little helmet and a tiny flashlight. My father and I walked the neighbourhood during air raid warnings, telling people to turn out their lights. I felt the power.

I remember when I was nine or ten school was dismissed early one Friday afternoon just before Christmas. I arrived home about 1:30 and saw my father's car was parked in the driveway. He had been away all week, so I raced up the stairs hoping to greet him. I flung open the front door, only to find him in the living room playing with a new electric train set. Our jaws both dropped when he saw me. "If you ever tell your mother, I'll kill you," he said sternly. I sat down with him on the floor and we played with that train for an hour. I never felt closer to my dad than I did that day. We had a secret, and we would share it with no one. On Christmas morning, I could have won an Academy Award for my performance in keeping our secret.

My mom Janet and dad Harvey in 1935.

My mother Janet was a wonderful person. She sold shoes pretty much all of her working life at Goodman's Department Store in New Glasgow. I remember her fitting shoes for two and three generations of people from Pictou County.

One weekend after I left home I recall visiting my mother and going into Goodman's to offer her a lift home. There was a third-generation shoe buyer in the store with her young mother. The little girl picked a pair of fancy shoes off the display counter and her mother said, "Do you want those, dear?" Before the kid could answer my mother said, "No, those shoes are not right

Me and Michael Connolly around 1950. My sister Beverly is leaning against our father's 1947 Chevy with some of the younger Connolly kids. My dad boarded with the Connolly family while surveying the No. 7 Highway.

for you. You need better support." The little girl had a fit when her mother told her, "Janet knows what's best for you. You can't have those shoes." She went away with the screaming girl in tow and my mother had made another conquest.

Janet could out-cook and out-bake any chef I've ever known. She made egg tarts, which are essentially butter tarts without the raisins. She used what is known as the Pictou County recipe for green tomato chow, passed down from her mother and my grandmother Agnes Fleming. Nanny Fleming used to lay out a big spread every year at Christmas, including the war years when food was rationed. I recall one Christmas when Beverly and I poured a few quarts of beer down the sink. We thought some of the men in the family were a little too drunk and didn't need any more booze. When my mother discovered what we'd done, she laughed and said it was their own fault – they shouldn't drink so much. My mother could drink anyone I knew under the table. I saw her at parties where the crowd would be passed out and Janet was still raring to go, calling them party-poopers.

Janet was a second mother to all my cousins, and a part-time psychologist for the family. She was an honest, hard-working person and she could swear like a trooper when pissed off. She had a stroke shortly after her eightieth birthday and never fully recovered. Janet Cameron died peacefully in December 1993.

My father was a quiet man who read every history book ever written. Harvey Gilmour Cameron was born in Montreal because his father and particularly his mother were living there at the time. His father and mother were a "mixed" marriage. Mary Elizabeth Murphy Cameron came from Ireland and was Catholic. Augustus Frank Cameron was Presbyterian, a descendant of the esteemed Alexander who came here on the *Hector*. The marriage was allowed as long as the children were raised in the Catholic church. There were three children from the marriage: my aunt Eileen, who remained a devout Catholic all her life; Harcourt, who never discussed religion, so I wasn't sure where he stood in the great scheme of things; and my father, who rejected the whole shootin' match. My dad would get a snoot full of rum on Christmas Eve and attend Midnight Mass at the Catholic church just for the fun of it.

I had a friend in grade school. Ronnie MacKenzie was a Catholic and I was a poor excuse for a Protestant. On Sunday afternoons Ronnie would participate in baseball games and all I could do was sit and watch. It was somehow un-Protestant to play. Come to think of it, all the corner stores in Pictou County would close on Sunday. They didn't dare open, lest the wrath of God would come down upon them. The one exception to all of that nonsense was Royal Sweets, a kind of soda shop that sold milkshakes and comic books. The Christian bullies didn't bother them. My father used to take us there on Sundays after Beverly and I attended Sunday school at St. Andrew's Presbyterian, known as the "Kirk" church. I was the class clown, even in Sunday school. I questioned everything, much to the frustration of the Sunday school teachers.

My father and mother rarely argued, except when Harvey arrived home late on a Friday night after drinking black rum and playing cards with his buddies. I remember one particular night. I have no idea what they were arguing about, but my mother's tongue was pretty caustic at times. I remember Dad saying, "I should have married your sister." She didn't speak to him for days after that one.

Dad's family didn't have things easy. His father, Augustus Frank Cameron, signed up for service in World War One and became a motorcycle dispatch rider. He was a staff sergeant in the Canadian Army Service Corps. He died after a collision with a horse. On August 12, 1917, my grandfather was speeding along a country road in France on his Triumph motorcycle. He was carrying a message from the front lines to where the generals used to hide, and as he rounded a sharp curve, there was a horse standing in the middle of the road. He couldn't avoid the collision. He was killed instantly. He's buried in France in a place called Gironde, near Bordeaux. I proudly bear his name. I didn't get the Augustus, but I got the Frank. And, by the way, it's Frank, not Francis.

I'm going to take a little detour here to recount something related to my grandfather. In 2014, I took a trip to England, France, Belgium, and Holland, visiting war cemeteries, Vimy Ridge, and Juno Beach. At the Juno Beach centre, I saw the film *They Walk With Us*, which showed a young Canadian family walking along Juno Beach. As the father tries to answer his son's question of "What happened here?" black and white footage of Canadian soldiers in full battle gear is superimposed on the screen. I'm not ashamed to say I cried watching this, and as I looked out over a very quiet beach ringed with apartment buildings and shops, I thought of those brave Canadians who stormed the beach on June 6, 1944. They kept coming while the German defences threw everything they could at them. I was never so proud to be a Canadian.

Unfortunately, I didn't get to see my grandfather's grave because it was way off the tour's beaten path, but when we visited Vimy Ridge, where many Canadians died in April 1917, I pictured Augustus Frank Cameron driving his motorcycle through those winding roads. I was very proud of him. Seeing where he actually was, imagining him there ... it was something I'll never forget.

My grandmother Mary Elizabeth brought up her three children – Harvey, Eileen, and Harcourt – alone after World War One. As a war widow, she received a government pension, which undoubtedly helped, but she was still a single mom raising small children – Harvey was ten, Eileen seven, and Harcourt four when Augustus and the horse met their shared fates. Raising a family through war and the Depression was no mean feat. She was proud of my father, who became an engineer like his father Augustus. Harcourt and Eileen also did very well for themselves, as you'll discover later in this book. My grandmother told my mother in the late '30s that she didn't want to live to see another war. Mary

Elizabeth died on August 31, 1939. World War Two began the next day. I was nine months old.

After World War Two, engineering jobs were hard to come by, but my father landed a job with an old Halifax construction firm, William Stairs, Son & Morrow. He was hired to survey the Number 7 Highway from Dartmouth to Sherbrooke. During the summers, he rented an old farmhouse on Spanish Ship Bay where I learned my sister Bev was afraid of garter snakes, particularly when I put them down her back.

On a couple of occasions, my mother, sister, and I travelled to Liscombe Mills where we found Rumleys' Lodge and Cabins. Mrs. Rumley churned her own butter from milk obtained from her own cow, and she made her own bread and goodies. It was like every day was a bake sale, and I was reaping the fruits of her labours. She also had an old Victrola, and I spent hours winding it up and playing "Abdul Abulbul Amir," an old song based on Percy French's 1877 poem about a Russian and a Turk. I pretended to be on the radio, even at that early age. Near the lodge was a rowboat. I couldn't swim (still can't), but I rowed that boat to a small island in the middle of Liscombe Harbour. That island contained millions of raspberries, blackberries (my favourite), and wild blueberries. They were ripe for the picking. My mother and I would do just that. I always ate whatever I picked.

The Liscombe River was full of eels, and some quiet evenings my dad and a bunch of his buddies would go eel fishing. My father would eat them, but I found them totally disgusting. I don't think my mother or sister were too crazy about them either.

My father suffered his first heart attack in 1950. It so damaged his heart that he never fully recovered. I remember the doctor's visits, the trip to the hospital, and the fact that I was scared out of my wits. They gave him glycerine pills, and for ten years he depended on those little suckers to ease his pain. I recall one day my mother asked him why he was missing so many pills. He replied he had dropped the bottle and wasn't able to retrieve some of them. The truth is he was taking too many, and he had the second severe heart attack in June 1960. I don't know if more advanced medical knowledge about heart conditions back then would've enabled doctors to give him more years or a more comfortable life. Maybe, maybe not.

He died in 1960, just a week before his first two grandchildren were born. My sister Bev gave birth to her first son, Ian, on July 14 and my then wife Diane gave birth to our daughter Seanna on July 15. My father loved children, and he would have loved his grandchildren, but he didn't live to see them. Harvey Gilmour Cameron died at age fifty-three. And he didn't get to meet his other grandsons. My son, Mark, and Beverly's second son, Steven, never got to know their grandfather, as I didn't know mine. I feel safe in the knowledge that Harvey Cameron would have loved his grandchildren, as I'm sure Augustus would have loved me and Beverly and all of his other grandchildren.

Harvey had worked at Goodman's Department store for a time, too, and they were very good to Janet when he died. In paying for the funeral, they lifted a great burden from her shoulders.

My sister Beverly and I fought like older sisters and younger brothers were supposed to do. Once, she pushed me down a flight of stairs. I took that with all the good grace and swear words I learned from my parents. I had some bruises, but I managed to come out of it with my body intact. There were times when Bev pushed me far beyond my level of tolerance. On one occasion, I sat on her and pummelled her until my mother dragged me off. She didn't bother me much after that, and I actually got to like her – hell, I even loved her. I still love her. Beverly managed a degree from Acadia University. I was so proud of her I even attended her graduation dance.

While at Acadia, she stayed with our uncle Harcourt Cameron. He was professor of geology at that great institution. When Professor Harcourt, or Harkey as the family called him, was in high school in New Glasgow, he was known as the Mighty Atom. He played rugby and he could run like the wind. While attending Acadia, he retained the title the Mighty Atom, and he could still run like the wind. Harcourt Cameron, like his brother Harvey, died at a young age.

The story is told of his expedition to Oak Island over two summers with students from his geology class. He came to the conclusion that there is no pirate treasure on Oak Island. What's more, there never was a pirate treasure on Oak Island. Those papers containing his conclusions are buried in a vault somewhere. The Nova Scotia government doesn't want anyone to see them, in case it kills what's left of our failing tourist industry. My uncle was also a mapmaker and regularly flew in high-altitude aircraft, mapping the east coast. I still have some contact with Peter Cameron, Harkey's oldest son.

Beverly met her husband, Fred Miles, at Acadia University. After graduation and marriage, she settled with Fred in Sydney, Cape Breton. There she took on a teaching job which turned into a lifetime career. I don't see Bev as often as I would like, although we keep in touch once a month by phone.

I don't think it would be an overstatement to say Beverly immersed herself in our Scottish culture. As we were growing up, she got involved in the Ceilidh

All dressed up and somewhere to go. Beverly and me, professionally photographed.

That's me with Glenda Arthurs, a member of the Ceilidh Girls Pipe Band who I had a huge crush on.

Girls Pipe Band. She played the bagpipes (as my late friend and mentor Rube Hornstein called them, the agony bags). I love the pipe band, but a lone piper playing on a hillside on a warm summer night is overrated. Also a dancer, Bev did the Highland Fling, the sword dance, the Seann Triubhas, and, of all things, the Irish Jig. She went to the Gaelic Mod every year in St. Ann's, Cape Breton, along with my father, mother, and me. She took Gaelic lessons. I'm pleased to know that in parts of Cape Breton the language is alive and well. By the way, Beverly was among the one hundred pipers who crossed the Canso Causeway linking mainland Nova Scotia with Cape Breton in 1955.

My father loved every minute of the Mod as we were swept up in the Scottish culture. Getting to St. Ann's before the TransCanada Highway was a challenge for his 1933 Plymouth with a 1946 engine. The director of the Gaelic college was Reverend A.W.R. MacKenzie. His wife (whose name escapes me) ran the gift shop and I used to work in the shop for no pay, selling ties and tams and tartans to the tourists. Mrs. MacKenzie (Bob and Doug's mother) seemed to like me. I turned on the charm and was one of her best sales persons. At least the stuff was made there and not some sweat shop in China.

The Gaelic college recently received a "royal" designation from the Queen, an insult to all those Scots who came to Canada after the Battle of Culloden, their culture having been summarily squashed by the English. My father's probably spinning in his grave over that one. (The negative reaction caused them, in March 2014, to drop the designation in day-to-day operations.)

Bev and Fred had a cottage bungalow on the Mira River, made famous by Allister MacGillivray's "Song for the Mira." I recall spending time there in the summer with them and their boys Ian and Steven, and my son and daughter, Mark and Seanna. (The kids are all now in their fifties.) We boiled water in large cauldrons and cooked many a lobster from Main-à-Dieu. Fred would sing, "Out on the Mira on warm afternoons, young men go fishing with black line and spoon." When he finished, we'd all have tears in our eyes. Fred was no Michael Bublé, but it is a beautiful song. I remember the summer of 1969. We watched Neil Armstrong make the big leap for mankind on the moon on a black and white TV set in my sister's cottage while munching on lobster sandwiches. Summers in Cape Breton are unlike anywhere else in the world.

2

New Glasgow and CKEC Radio

My media career began in grade five at Acadia school in New Glasgow. Instead of concentrating on boring school subjects, I began a scandal sheet. It was mostly gossip and downright lies about fellow students and teachers. It was something like the *National Enquirer* or those other trash tabloids you see in every supermarket. I only showed it to a select group of friends. I never made a nickel from it.

It was during this period that I began to fantasize about a career in radio. New Glasgow didn't have a radio station at that time. We listened to CFCY Charlottetown and CJFX in Antigonish. CJFX was owned by J. Clyde Nunn, a.k.a. the old-timer. My father and I got a great kick out of him as he did the voice of an older guy playing a lot of Scottish music. J. Clyde had a son named Jim, who I would work with later at the CBC. I remember a couple of guys coming to New Glasgow from Antigonish in the late '40s as the town was celebrating its seventy-fifth anniversary. One of them was the late Danny Gallivan, who coined a number of classic hockey phrases when he called the play on CBC out of Montreal. I'm sure it was a cannonading drive from Antigonish to New Glasgow. I followed him around all day, hoping he might say, "Wanna be on the radio, kid?" But he didn't. I was devastated.

If I had a career other than radio or TV it would be as a movie projectionist. I know that sounds funny, but I love movies. When I was a kid, my mother or father would give me fifty cents on a Saturday afternoon and I and my pals would head for the Academy Theatre in New Glasgow for a movie marathon. It was fifteen cents to get in. Coke was a nickel, popcorn was another nickel and licorice nibs rounded out the treat category, also a nickel. This left me twenty cents for more nutritious fare: penny candy and Hatfield's chips. About one o'clock things would get rolling with a Three Stooges comedy followed by a serial and a Bowery Boys movie starring Leo Gorcey and Huntz Hall, and the *pièce de résistance*, a Western, or duster as we used to call them, starring Johnny Mac Brown, Hopalong Cassidy, Roy Rogers, or Gene Autry. Autry was the only cowboy who could fall off his horse without dropping his hat.

As I got older and more sophisticated, I used to attend the Roseland Theatre. The Roseland became famous for its treatment of the black community in New Glasgow. The local blacks were not allowed to sit downstairs in the Roseland and were forced to sit in the balcony. It was insidious racism which I didn't understand at the time, but it soon became clear that New Glasgow was no better than the southern United States. In 1946, Viola Desmond, a Halifax native who was in New Glasgow during a business trip, decided to take in a movie while waiting for her car to be repaired. She took a seat on the main floor, which was for whites only and cost more. When told to move, she refused, was arrested, dragged out of the theatre, spent the night in jail, was fined twenty dollars, and convicted of tax evasion, based on the one-cent difference between the balcony and main floor seats. The Nova Scotia Supreme Court upheld the conviction. Many years after her death, Viola received a free pardon, and in 2014 the provincial government apolgized for her wrongful conviction.

At the Roseland, I'd see such blockbusters as *Blackboard Jungle* and *On the Waterfront*. Marlon Brando won an Academy Award for *On the Waterfront* in 1954. He is one of my favourite actors of all time. My favourite Christmas movie of all time is *A Christmas Carol* with Alastair Sim. Ted Turner's company colourized it a few years ago, but I refuse to watch the phony colour version. Let's hope *On the Waterfront* is never colourized. If it is, I shall personally strangle Ted Turner. These movies were shot in black and white and were meant to be gritty. I watch a lot of movies to this day on Turner Classic Movies and Silver Screen Classics.

We couldn't go to movies on Sunday because the Christian bullies in government had passed the Lord's Day Act, and it said you couldn't see anything mildly entertaining on Sunday. So most Christians stayed home and played poker.

I loved my hometown, and I still have a soft spot in my heart for the people of Pictou County. While in high school, I worked for a couple of weeks at Sobeys on Provost Street. It was a few doors down from McCarron's Restaurant where I spent time eating chips with gravy and sipping real fountain Coke. I tried sniffing Coke but the bubbles kept going up my nose.

I had a short stint in army cadets in high school. Apparently, if you were male and in the three high grades you were expected to join army cadets. I marched, I presented arms, I ordered arms (although I already had two), and I was probably the worst cadet ever to darken the door of New Glasgow High. I went to cadet camp in Debert one summer. I didn't stay long. I didn't agree with the idiots there who painted testicles with black shoe polish, although they didn't do it to me. Other things were done by fourteen-year-olds with the minds of five-year-olds that I didn't agree with, so I fled the place and never went back. I was bullied and called a sissy and every other nasty name the school jocks could think of, but I didn't give a rat's ass.

While in high school I took a swing at rugby, but couldn't grasp the rules of the game, such as passing the ball back instead of forward. Since I weighed about 125 pounds soaking wet, I soon came to the conclusion I was too young to die, and that rugby is indeed a stupid game. I was a pretty good skater, but I never played hockey, except the odd game of shinny on a frozen pond near my house. Our PT instructor, John Brother MacDonald, asked me if I would like to learn the fine art of refereeing. I said sure, and pretty soon I was on my skates every Saturday at the trusty New Glasgow Stadium. I started at eight a.m. and finished at four p.m. I put up with swearing kids and insane hockey dads for seven hours, but I was wearing that striped sweater and blew the whistle. I felt the power ... again!

Growing up in New Glasgow had its advantages. In a small town (about 10,000 people), everybody knows everybody. That can be good or bad, depending on how you look at it. In the days before shopping malls, people shopped downtown. There were two main streets in the downtown, Provost and Archimedes. Provost was the main drag and young men used to endlessly drive around the block hoping to score with a member of the opposite sex. You could afford to do that in your V8, which got ten miles per gallon. But gas was twenty-nine cents a gallon. The stores had some odd opening and closing times. You didn't open on Sundays for fear of being stricken with a bolt of lightning from Up There. Mondays and Tuesdays nine to five, Wednesdays were half-days from nine to twelve noon, Thursdays and Fridays nine to five, and Saturday nine to nine. On Friday nights the evangelists would set up shop in a vacant lot near McCarron's Restaurant to generally tell us we were going to hell and we should be born again and be saved and all that stuff.

One Saturday night I was walking across the bridge heading for home when I heard footsteps behind me. Someone was walking very quickly and wanted to catch up to me. When he did, he grabbed me by the butt and said, "Wanna go into the bushes and fool around?" I took a swing at him and he took off like a shot. I was fifteen at the time, and it was my first encounter with a gay person. We didn't call them gays. In those days gay meant happy. I won't tell you what we used to call them, other than perverts. Anyway, guess who this guy turned out to be? Yep. It was Mister Evangelist himself.

Speaking of the west side of New Glasgow, not far from our house every spring we witnessed what had become known as the river rat massacre. Let me explain. I always had a cat growing up and even to this day, and we had an old Tom named Fluffy who was the biggest cat I have ever known. You'd think a cat with such an original name would be a real pussycat. Nope. Fluffy loved my father, was lukewarm to me and my sister, and loathed my mother, even though she was the one who fed him the most. And every spring, the river rats who spent the winter hibernating in the riverbank would leave their nests and come look for food. Few of them made it to the street. The gauntlet of neighbourhood cats would make mincemeat out of the rodents and the town didn't have to do a thing except clean up what was left of them.

The family lived in Trenton for a short time, and one cloudy night in the autumn, I can't remember the year, a bunch of guys, including myself, decided to disrupt the home and school meeting at Trenton High School, not far from my house. We sneaked into the parking lot of the school and let the air out of every tire on every car in the lot. We were eventually ratted out by one of our number and we all gathered at the police station. We were brought into an interrogation room individually and grilled under the lukewarm lights until we confessed. Our parents had to make restitution for all the valve covers we took off the tires. It must have cost them at least a dollar each. I was severely reprimanded by my mother. She was the disciplinarian in the family.

I'm not sure about today's educational system in Nova Scotia. It lacks the power to teach our children how to attack problems. Math and science are done by the computer, English is being killed by technology (i.e. texting), and we are so close to our neighbours next door, we are almost forced to speak and write American, not English. Young people are going to call me a fuddy-duddy and really old, but I don't care. Reading, writing, and arithmetic used to be the grounding to continue down the academic road. Reading now means computer, but these machines (as great as they may be) can't teach you how to write. Arithmetic is now math, and all you need is a calculator. You are not taught to think for yourself.

Well, I was. I had a marvelous English teacher in high school. His name was Wilfred Burchill, and he knew a class clown when he saw one. He encouraged me to embrace the great classics in English literature. We would do Shakespeare in class. He would invariably pick me for two reasons. He wanted me to excel in English because he knew what my ambitions were. And if I were involved in the play, I wouldn't be able to make smart remarks from the sidelines. There are very few Wilfred Burchills left in the world.

During my time in New Glasgow High School, the principal was L.M. Rhodenizer, who distinguished himself on Juno Beach on June 6, 1944. He wasn't a happy camper when I rejected army cadets. Verna Horne taught history and she could kick you out of class without missing a beat. Here's an example: "Christopher Columbus had three ships, the *Nina*, Frank Cameron get out, the *Pinta*, and the *Santa Maria*." Duffy MacDonald taught math, mostly by intimidation. If you weren't paying attention, a piece of chalk or a blackboard brush would sail through the air in your general direction. It usually got your attention. We had a French teacher, who was part of a sister team at New Glasgow High. Iona Olding couldn't speak French, but she was charged with teaching a bunch of Anglo kids Parisian French. We learned grammar and how to form a sentence, but that was it.

Hugh Townsend was one of my classmates through school. His dad owned a car dealership in New Glasgow and Hugh and I got along pretty well. Hughie (as I called him) had the bug. Not the radio bug. He had the writing bug and the sports bug. He wanted to be a sports writer and that's just what he did. Hugh went on to distinguish himself with the *New Glasgow Evening News* and later the Halifax *Chronicle Herald*, where he spent much of his career in the sports-writing trenches. Hugh is still making a contribution to sports writing with the *Pictou Advocate*.

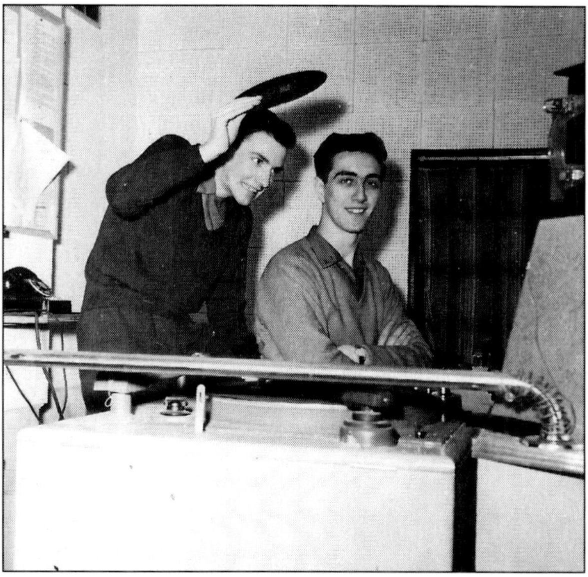

I'm the one holding the vinyl over Don Campbell at CKCL Truro in 1958. We worked together at CKCL and CKEC New Glasgow. Don, a New Glasgow native, went on to CJCB Sydney where he toiled for several years. Don died of throat cancer in the late 1980s.

John James (Jim) Grant was two years older than me but attended New Glasgow High School. He went on to have a distinguished career in the military, becoming a brigadier general. He lived in New Glasgow not far from me. His father was a mayor of New Glasgow and now Jim is Nova Scotia's lieutenant governor.

During the last two years in high school I co-hosted a radio show for high school students with my best friend, Alexander (Sandy) Hoyt. Sandy was a year younger than me, but we had that same thirst for radio. We had a set-up in his basement with a couple of record players and a phony microphone and we played at radio for hours. We would've done anything to get on the air. When the opportunity came to do a show on New

Glasgow's radio station, CKEC, where we volunteered as gofers, we jumped at the chance. We weren't paid a cent, but we were in our own little world and didn't care. The show went on for two hours on a Saturday afternoon. Pretty soon, it was extended by an hour, and eventually we ran the station until midnight. The staff took the day off. We played the latest hits by the Four Aces and Tony Bennett and made up stuff about all the high schools in Pictou County.

I remember going to Sandy's father's hardware store and observing the farmers coming in from rural Pictou County and listening to their conversations. I still recall one saying to the other, "How's the new truck workin', Phil?" And Phil's reply: "I just come up from Piedmont with a load of shit." Piedmont was in Antigonish County and the shit was fertilizer. There were so many times Sandy and I would look at each other and say, "Will we ever get a job in this business? Or will you own a hardware store and will I be your friendly neighbourhood engineer?" With respect to our fathers, I'm glad we went the way we did.

In an article about Sandy for *Close Up* magazine in 1984, Joanne Tory makes reference to his love of radio and quotes him as recalling "that great theatre of the mind, listening to *Our Miss Brooks*, *The Great Gildersleeve*, or the *Lux Radio Theatre* ... It was great food for a child's imagination ... the wonderful things they did with words." Our shared love for both radio and language – no wonder Sandy and I were best friends.

In 1955, the owner of CKEC, Jim Cameron (no relation), offered me a full-time job at the station. I didn't give it a second thought. Pretty soon I was making $27.50 a week and all the records I could steal. I went out of my way to please Old Balderdash, a guy named Howard MacLean, who was program director. He used the word "balderdash" in lieu of dirty words. I had the radio bug and there was nothing my mom or dad could do about it.

Jim Cameron was typical of radio station owners at the time. If he didn't like a certain type of music, it didn't get played. But that didn't stop the boys and girls of CKEC from playing that new-fangled rock and roll music. We tried calling Bill Haley Bill McHaley. Jim saw through that in a heartbeat. He sometimes would come into the station at night to confront the culprit who might have played an Elvis song. He'd roll those Celtic eyes and say, "Laddie, you've been playing that cowboy music again." He called us Laddie because he couldn't remember any of our names.

I hosted daily radio shows and still remember doing an interview with the Crew Cuts, a group of Toronto choir boys who had a number of big hits in the mid '50s. You'll probably recognize "Sh-Boom," a second-rate version of a black doo-wop song by the Chords. The original recording wasn't released in Canada until 1956.

During my career in New Glasgow and Truro and later at CHNS, I played a lot of records by Pat Boone. Like the Crew Cuts, Pat was notorious for recording covers of black singers and groups. Racism reared its ugly head in radio in those days. Black R&B and doo-wop groups had a problem getting their material played on the air even in the so-called enlightened northern states. And Canada was at the mercy of the record companies based in the U.S., who treated their Canadian subsidiaries and partners like crap. Fats Domino had a hit recording in the southern U.S. with "Ain't That a Shame." Pat Boone's handlers saw an opening and released his perfectly awful version of the song. It went to number one. To this very day, I will not play the Boone version on the air. The previously mentioned Crew Cuts did a pretty crappy version of "Earth Angel," an original recording by the Penguins, an African-American group

There were other Caucasian cover artists who made a fortune doing cover versions of black songs. The good news was: the songwriters were mostly non-Caucasian and they made a few bucks as well. When record buyers in the northern U.S. and Canada realized what was going on, they began rejecting this cover stuff. Pat Boone then switched to ballads such as "April Love" and "Love Letters in the Sand." His career continued and his popularity remained solid for a number of years.

Every morning around 10:30, CKEC used to feature a BBC transcription series called *Love and Marriage*. One morning I cued up the big disc on the turntable and blurted out the intro. "Stay tuned for" and the BBC announcer was supposed to come in and say, with his articulate and meaningful voice, "*Love and Marriage*." Unfortunately, the turntable malfunctioned and wouldn't start. After a slight pause, I said (not realizing my mike was still open), "You rotten slut." Adding insult to injury, a woman called the station and asked, "Did they change the name of the show?"

The radio and TV audiences can be hilarious. One night at CHNS we had a power failure and the generator didn't kick in because it was flooded. A woman called and asked, "Is the station off the air?"

"Yes," said I. "We've had a power failure."

Came the reply, "Well, why don't you tell people you're off the air?"

My response could have scripted a similar *WKRP* episode: "How can we announce that we're off the air when we're off the air?"

Another goodie was the night cable TV had a power failure and didn't have emergency power. I was sitting in the CBC newsroom watching the hockey game when this call came in. "Typical CBC goes off the air in the middle of a playoff game!" grumbled the caller.

I said, "No, sir, we're not off the air. The game is still on."

The guy said, "Well, how come it went blank?"

"Do you have cable, sir?"

"Yeah, what's that got to do with it?"

"Can you get any other channels, sir?"

"No, I can't. What did you do to my set?"

"Nothing, sir. You have lost your cable feed. You'll have to call the cable company."

"Isn't there anyone there that can help me?"

"No, you need to take it up with cable."

"What's their number?"

"It's in the phone book."

Final statement: "Typical CBC."

One night after I had finished the weather, I got this call. "Is this the weatherman?"

"Yes, sir."

"Whal, you all said the temperature tomorrow would be twenty-six degrees. That seems awful cold."

"No, sir, it's Celsius."

"What the hell is Celsius?"

"It's a better way of measuring temperatures and wind speeds and all that stuff."

"Whal, Ahm from Texas and we work in American degrees."

"There's no such thing as American degrees. You'd be talking about Fahrenheit."

"Never heard of it. I only know American degrees, and I think that other stuff is French. I never had much use for the French."

"Y'all have a nice day, sir."

If the truth be known, the U.S. adopted the metric system before Canada, but they never put it into practice. And there are Canadians who stubbornly cling to the old Imperial system. Many of them think metric is a French plot to take over the world.

After CKEC shut off for the night, a few of us would gather and make tapes, mostly takeoffs of other radio shows. These tapes never got to air. They were filthy. I remember one in particular doing a send-up of an American radio show called *Can You Top This?* The idea was for panellists to tell jokes and let the audience decide who told the funniest story. Our version was called Can You F— This? We told the dirtiest jokes you'd ever want to hear. Sandy was wickedly funny – he was always the glib one and I could hardly keep up with him when he was ad libbing. We played canned laughter and applause. And our production careers were born.

I'm proud of my production skills. I would come into CKEC on my day off (Sunday) to produce a radio show for Dr. Carrie Best (1903-2001), the first African-Nova Scotian to host a weekly radio show in the province. Her program, *The Quiet Corner*, ran from 1952 to 1964. She was also the founder of *The Clarion*, Nova Scotia's first black-owned and -published newspaper. Small wonder she was later inducted into the Order of Canada and awarded the Order of Nova Scotia.

During the mid '50s racism ran rampant in Pictou County. I never saw Carrie get angry, but despite being mild-mannered, she was a feisty woman who stood up to the white establishment. She used her considerable intelligence and influence to break down the barriers between the races. Black people couldn't get their hair done at white barber shops. They had to sit in the balcony at the Roseland Theatre. They couldn't even go into some restaurants with their white friends. In the U.S. racism was out in the open. Not here. It was hidden behind closed doors. That's the most insidious kind of racial tension. I loved Carrie Best.

One Sunday after the show, I went home for dinner with my parents. The radio was on, and a new guy was on the air. His name was Eldridge MacDonald, and he wasn't quite familiar with the control board. In the middle of a hymn there were ten seconds of some of the most creative curse words I had ever heard. My mother was shocked and my father was laughing so hard he could barely stay in his chair. I grabbed the phone and called Eldridge. The hymn was still playing as he picked up the phone and said (still with the mike open), "Hello, CKEC." I tried to whisper, "Eldridge, shut off your mike." But before I got the words out Eldridge said, "Thank God it's you, Frank. I can't hear a f—king thing. How the f—k do I get this speaker to work?" I'll save the remaining profanities for another time, but I finally convinced him to turn off the mike.

John Brother MacDonald was not only a hell of a hockey player in his day, but he became the head P.T. instructor for all the schools in New Glasgow. The New Glasgow Stadium hosted a huge P.T. Day once a year, and I remember showing up in my white T-shirt and white shorts and going through the paces with three hundred kids. I looked like an emaciated character from a zombie movie.

One of John Brother's other jobs was sportscaster for CKEC. He would do a morning sportscast and then tape one for the noon hour before he went to the schools for the day. He used to ask the morning crew to whom he should refer on the tape. So the tape would be: "Thank you, Frank Cameron, and good afternoon, sports fans." Once in a while when I got to introduce the tape I would say, "Here's John Brother MacDonald to say thank you, Frank Cameron, and good afternoon, sports fans." Start the tape and he would say it. I loved doing that stuff.

John Brother ended his sportscasts with a simple expression: "We can't all be good athletes, but we can all be good sports." I have tried my best to live up to that motto. I don't embrace the philosophy of many of my fellow Canadians and our neighbours to the south, which is "It doesn't matter how you play the game, as long as you win" and "Winning is everything." I think about John Brother as I watch Olympic coverage on television. Olympians want the gold medal, but most of them are just happy to be there representing their country, and those countries should be applauding their athletes no matter where they place in the standings.

There were a couple of things about CKEC that could be considered "odd." The station was located in the old Eastern Chronicle building beside the railway tracks. Those tracks were part of the main line to Sydney, and every morning just as the eight a.m. news hit the air, a trainload of coal cars would go rushing by. It shook the building to its core, and the noise was deafening.

The other "funny" thing was the toilet. You see, the only place to put the new plumbing was in the record library, which gave the second floor a washroom, but you had to go through the master control room (MCR) to use it. Guys would go walking through the MCR while one of us was on the air. Soon you would hear grunting sounds and then the flush. Sir Thomas Crapper would have been proud.

3

Truro, A Town Without Strong Drink

In 1956 I spread my wings and moved to the town of Truro. There, I met another future activist in the African-Nova Scotian community. He was in high school at the time. He was Burnley "Rocky" Jones and I didn't get to know him until we both moved to Halifax. Rocky became a lawyer and was instrumental in bringing a wakeup call to the people of Halifax concerning the treatment of black people. Rocky went to law school at Dalhousie University in the early '90s and became an advocate for prisoners in Dorchester Penitentiary. A founding member of the Black United Front, the National Black Coalition of Canada, and the Dalhousie Law School Indigenous Blacks and Mi'kmaq Program, among others, he stood up for human rights and was a champion of indigenous blacks and Mi'kmaq people. He died in 2013 and we are a lot poorer for his loss. He once told me, "Frank, I still have miles to go."

CKCL in Truro was the creation of Art Manning and Sid Bernasconi. The control boards were homemade and the station was staffed with some of the most talented radio people you'll ever find. A Brit by the name of Derek Upton (even sounds British) was the sales manager and he set the town on its ear with block programming. That's personality radio and even the Halifax stations hadn't caught on to this one. Block programming means the station's day is broken into a series of blocks, each block hosted by a different personality. Radio has since degenerated into nameless radio hosts who might as well be robots. We began to play rock and roll and the kids loved it. Actually, I was only eighteen that year and I loved it too.

That first summer in Truro I made a new friend in the person of Ken Bagnell. He was studying at Pine Hill Divinity School in Halifax and came to CKCL for the summer. I remember doing an evening shift one night. Ken happened to pop in and took a phone call from a woman who wanted to hear a song, which I promptly played. Ken also happened to get her phone number and it was agreed that when I finished my shift Ken and I and Ken's divinity pal Louie would go to her house and ... like ... hang out.

We arrived at her house about 10:30 and we were welcomed by a number of young women. There was no orgy, but Ken used his skills as a hypnotist to put a couple of these women "under." He made them do some funny stuff but stopped short at the removal of clothing or any other naughty bits. A fun time was had by all, but nobody scored, including me. I had the opportunity to work with Ken again at the CBC. Ken Bagnell went on to become executive editor of a glossy magazine published by the United Church, known as the *Observer*.

CKCL had an early afternoon show, *Call For Help*. The audience would present a problem to the host, who in turn would do a shout-out to the audience looking for solutions to the problem. Doug Freeman was the program director at the station and the host of the program. I went along for the ride. One day, a woman called and asked, "How do I get grass stains off my wedding dress?" I said to Doug (off the air), "Gee, I guess she couldn't wait for the honeymoon." He cracked up. I cracked up. Nobody knew why in hell we were laughing. We milked that one for months.

Doug Freeman bought CKEC from Jim Cameron and it's now on FM (what isn't?) and being run by Doug's son. Another graduate of CKEC is Anna Maria Tremonti, who now hosts the popular CBC Radio show *The Current*. I don't know Anna Maria Tremonti, but I love her work.

I was in Truro during both Springhill mine disasters. The first one in 1956 meant a lot because people depended on CKCL to get the latest news from the mining town. The Amherst station CKDH was not yet on the air, so we were the closest radio station to the mine. CKCL stayed on twenty-four hours a day until the crisis was over.

It happened again in 1958. I remember one evening about eight o'clock walking past the UPI printer as the bells went off. A bulletin was imminent and, sure enough, a terse message read, "Bump in Springhill mine. Miners trapped. More later." I remember running up the stairs to put something on the air, thinking ... not again. The phones began ringing off the hook. "Hi, this is ABC News in New York. Can you tell us what's happening in Springhill?" By this time, Canadian Press and Broadcast News were printing items. I ripped them off the printer and read them verbatim in a report for ABC. They didn't know, the poor devils!

The second incident in Springhill brought a new name to the public relations field. Arnie Patterson was the public relations spokesman for Dominion Coal Company, owners of the Springhill mine. During the 1960s he started Dartmouth's first radio station. It was a dawn-to-dusk operation known as CFDR, and it appealed to the silver-haired crowd. It operated from sunup to sundown because of some stupid deal that was made with the U.S. where our stations couldn't interfere with theirs, particularly at night when AM radio was king. At the time the deal was made, Canada got the short end of the stick and the U.S. walked all over us with their zillion radio stations as opposed to our fifty. Anyway, CFDR thrived and was doing well until the audience literally died off.

I recall a meeting with Harry Steele (who bought CFDR from Arnie) and me and my old pal Gary MacPherson. Gary was working for Harry and they wanted to know how I felt about CFDR going Top 40. I can't recall what I told them, but I remember thinking, "This ain't gonna work." And sure enough, it didn't. CFDR eventually became KIXX Country, and lasted for quite a while. It was playing classic country but then along came the switch to FM and the station became another outlet chasing the pimple crowd. Sad.

As I write this, I am working with a couple of CFDR alumni at Seaside FM. Paul Mahar hosts a number of programs at the Eastern Passage station, and we've been friends for more years than I can count. Gail Rice is a multi-talented sports-oriented woman who I have also known for many years. She's only as big as a minute, but she has spent many years on air and became program director at CFDR. *And* she coaches basketball, for heaven's sake.

While toiling in Truro in 1958, I got a call from CCA (Colchester County Academy) or Truro High School asking if I would referee a high school hockey game. I'd never done a high school game, but I said sure, I'll do it. I reported to the old Truro rink at the appointed time, donned my skates and my zebra sweater, and hit the ice with my trusty whistle. It seems CCA was playing East Pictou Rural High School. The East Pictou team contained one Lowell MacDonald, future NHL star and a guy who came up through the very hockey system that spawned the likes of me as a referee. There were two minutes left in the third period. The score was tied and Lowell was in on the Truro net all alone when he was tripped. That called for a penalty shot. Lowell took the shot, scored, and East Pictou won the game.

Now, Truro was, is, and forever shall be a wonderful town with wonderful people. But they're rabid hockey fans. I left the rink that day holding my skates over my head, threatening to carve the first person to lay a hand on me. It was the first and last time I refereed a hockey game in Truro. Lowell MacDonald went on to play for the Detroit Red Wings, the Los Angeles Kings, and the Pittsburgh Penguins during the '60s and '70s. He played his last two years with a painful shoulder injury and retired in 1978.

A word about Lowell MacDonald's dad. He was the ultimate hockey dad. When Lowell was playing in the New Glasgow Stadium during his minor hockey days, his father showed up for every game. He used to stand behind the mesh and shout encouragement to his son. He was never rude to the referees or other officials. He didn't shout obscenities at the other team, and was an all around gentleman.

Too bad you can't say that about many hockey dads. Many of them live vicariously through their sons, and they stand by the boards and shout childish epithets at the referees and anyone who'll listen, lest they annoy their upcoming Sidney Crosby. When I refereed, I remember a guy literally running up and down the boards calling me every rotten name he could think of, while his son skated with his head down (bad move) hoping no one would recognize him. I stopped the game and had the police remove the guy. Referees then were an abused bunch. They still are an abused bunch.

Some fathers (I'm not making this up) would wait for the referees to leave their dressing room. We would be confronted by these guys who would threaten to beat the crap out of us. They were mostly thirty-somethings with the minds of twelve-year-olds. All of this is still happening today and it's getting worse. The hockey moms have joined the parade and they are just as bad as the dads. Minor hockey is great fun for the kids. But that's it. It's supposed to be fun. Young referees are quitting because of the situation. These dads believe that because they pay a lot of money for ice time and equipment, this gives them the right to bully the league and its referees. It doesn't.

When I arrived in Truro in 1956 I was too young to drink ... legally. You couldn't find a strong drink in Truro anyway, unless you went to the liquor store or a bootlegger. House parties in Truro during the late '50s were legendary, sometimes lasting for days. I hosted record hops every Saturday night at the Legion. All the teens showed up at these hops.

In 1957 I began dating a Truro girl named Diane Bigsby. We married in 1959 and had two children. Seanna was born in 1960, Mark in 1962. Diane's brother Austin was a hell of a musician. He got his teaching certificate from the Nova Scotia Teachers College in Truro and soon he was a fully fledged teacher. He ended his career as a high school principal in British Columbia, where he died from pancreatic cancer in 2014. I remember attending a Gordon Lightfoot concert at the old Capitol Theatre in Halifax with Austin. He was slightly inebriated and was making rude remarks to a rather large man as we waited in the lineup. But the guy wasn't having any part of it. He dismissed Austin's insults as the ravings of a pissed individual. I didn't want to get involved because the guy could have wiped the floor with both of us.

Austin and sax player Lane Francis formed a band called the Novatones. Roddie Norrie was the drummer and Wayne Mills played bass. Roddie married my wife Diane's best friend Eleanor, who later became an MLA and served in the Nova Scotia Legislature from 1993 to 1998. Roddie's father founded the Noranda gold mines in Quebec (the Nor is for Norrie) and his mother was appointed to the senate by Pierre Trudeau. Roddie's sister married into the frozen food family in New Brunswick known as the McCains. In 1994 Margaret Norrie McCain became the first female lieutenant governor of New Brunswick. Her daughter Eleanor McCain is now a recording artist and a very good vocalist. She's just released *Runaway*.

Wayne worked for his dad at his service station in Truro. One fine summer weekend we travelled to Halifax to make a recording of our song "Mary Lee." I helped to write the lyrics, such as they were, and Wayne Mills and Lane Francis wrote the music. I think we sold three copies. Years later, Wayne was in Bangor, Maine. He was shopping at Borders, the equivalent to our Chapters, when he came across a CD titled *Early Canadian Rockers*.

Guess what was on the disc? Yep. There was "Mary Lee" by the Novatones. I still have that disc.

Another musician I met in Truro was Chalmers Doane. He was a high school chum of my future brother-in-law Austin, and he played in the Colchester County Academy band. Chalmers attended the now defunct Nova Scotia Teachers College after high school. From there he received a Bachelor of Music Education from Boston College in 1967, where he studied the trombone. He was Supervisor of Music in the Halifax School Board from 1967 to 1984, and taught every kid in Halifax and beyond how to play, of all things, the ukulele. He returned to Truro in 1984 where he became Professor of Music Education at NSTC, his alma mater. He retired in 1993, but his son Creighton and his daughter Melanie carry on the music tradition in the family. Melanie and Creighton both live in Toronto and they can play the ukulele, but Creighton is an award-winning drummer and Melanie enjoys great success with her beautiful voice and equally beautiful songs. She has appeared in several Neptune Theatre productions and even made it to Broadway in *The Buddy Holly Story*.

In the summer of 1958, as CKCL was operating from temporary studios at the Truro curling club, the hammer came down at the radio station. It seems the owner's wife was playing bridge one night and she and her friends decided CKCL was playing far too much of that awful rock and roll. So out went rock and in came scratchy discs of Guy Lombardo and Mantovani. This was sanctioned by the program director, Jack Armstrong, who was a jazz musician and organist. He didn't like rock music anyway.

My best friend and kindred spirit, Sandy Hoyt.

While working in the Hubtown I kept in touch with my friend Sandy Hoyt, who had taken a job with CKEN in Kentville, part of the Annapolis Valley radio group. On a few occasions I took the train from Truro to Kentville. It was a combined freight and passenger service operated by the DAR (Dominion Atlantic Railway), a subsidiary of Canadian Pacific. The trip took three hours, but it was fun. That line, like most rail lines in Atlantic Canada, has long ago been closed. Canada is the only country in the world that closes rail lines. Politicians fall over each other to improve the highways and close the rail links. It flies in the face of Confederation. But I digress.

Sandy eventually made his way to Toronto where he made a name for himself. He was lured back to Nova Scotia for a short time when a new radio station opened in Port Hawkesbury. He was manager of that station for a while. Then it was back to Toronto where he finished his career. He hosted the Santa Claus Parade in Toronto for years on television. When the CBC cancelled *The Don Messer Show*, it was picked up by CHCH in Hamilton. The host was none other than my best friend, Sandy Hoyt.

I mentioned earlier that Sandy and I were really alike, and we got up to stuff both on air and off. I'm going to jump ahead in time a bit here. One year, Diane and I went camping in Maine with Sandy and his wife Alice. Alice was seven months pregnant with their first child, Allison, but she was a gamer. When we were looking for the campground, we stopped along the old highway and there was an elderly gentleman whittling on the porch of a general store (absolutely true). We asked for directions to the campground. He told us, "You're looking for Edmonds Pahk." I said, "How do we get to Edmonds Pahk?" I was chastised by those in the car for making fun of him, but I retorted, "Seriously, I thought that was the name of the place." How naïve was I? Let me count the ways (with apologies to Elizabeth Barrett Browning).

When we finally found Edmonds Pahk, we put our car beside a vehicle with New Jersey plates and while we were setting up the tent, two boys about eleven or twelve approached us. They were hesitant to speak, but finally one of them asked, "Do ... you ... speak ... English?" That's when our sick sense of humour kicked in. Sandy and I looked at each other, shrugged our shoulders, and in very bad French said, "Comprend Anglais?" The boys turned quickly and one said to the other, "See, I told you Canadians didn't speak English!" A sad commentary on American ignorance (even at twelve) and two DJs with questionable humour (well beyond twelve). The good news is, they somehow knew we were

Canadians. We could've been on an episode of "Talking to Americans." Rick Mercer would have been proud. I didn't camp much after that. My idea of roughing it was staying in a motel with black and white television. Sandy died of brain cancer in 2002. I loved him and still miss him and all the fun we had together.

In 1959 I applied for a job at the CBC in Halifax. In those days you were supposed to do an apprenticeship in Sydney before coming to the big city. I got the job, but I didn't go to Sydney.

So I was unemployed for a few months. I even picked up a few cheques. But in March of that year, CHNS came into my life. It seems the station was looking for a host for the morning show, and I had lunch in Truro with the program director, Fred Arenburg. I was about to be hired by one of Nova Scotia's oldest radio stations, and things were looking up.

4

THE WEIRD AND THE WONDERFUL: CHNS

The morning show on CHNS in 1959 was called *Life Begins at 960*. Clever title, but the show sucked. CHNS was badly behind in the radio ratings. CJCH was killing it with *Breakfast With Bill*, hosted by the late great Bill Fulton. CHNS had an illustrious history. It came on the air in 1926 and some of its stodgy past was coming back to haunt it.

When I did the morning show on CHNS, it went from six a.m. to nine a.m. I couldn't play Peggy Lee. She was considered nightclub music. There was a lot of Mitch Miller and any other music of that ilk you could think of. I called it sliced bread music. It was boring as hell. But that wasn't the end of my day. At 9:30 I hosted a quiz show with Clive Schaefer called *Right or Wrong*, where we called a listener and made a statement. He or she (mostly she) would tell us whether the statement was right or wrong. Clive would do the questions and I sat there with my trusty xylophone. When

I sounded a couple of notes, that meant the person on the phone could go for the jackpot.

One day in late 1959 we were talking to a listener on the phone. This incident is burned into my memory and I remember it like it was yesterday. The conversation went like this:

Clive says, "Potato chips grow wild in Ireland."

Mrs. Smith says, "Right."

Clive says, "Wrong." The xylophone dings.

Clive says, "Hey, Mrs. Smith, you have a chance to win the treasure hunt!"

Mrs. Smith screams with excitement. "I'm on the treasure hunt! I'm on the treasure hunt!"

"Yes," says Clive. "We've been making quite a few treasure hunt calls this morning."

At least that's what he meant to say. He really put the "c" where the "h" should have been and the "h where the "c" should have been. Dead silence. I laughed so hard I had to leave the studio. I looked up at the control room and saw a disembodied hand grasping the turntable. Our technician, Herm Fullerton, was so shocked he fell off his chair.

Fred Arenburg embarked on a great adventure in late 1960. He travelled to three or four American cities and a couple of Canadian ones just to listen to the radio. When he returned, it was decided that CHNS would be going Top 40, or Top 60 as we called it. The manager, Gerry Redmond, resigned. He couldn't get over the fact that CHNS was killing the morning march – you marched around the breakfast table to the beat of military bands, threw up your porridge and went back to bed claiming nine o'clock sickness or marched out the door and off to school without hurling. It was an anachronism that went over big in the 1930s and '40s but had outlived its usefulness, let alone most of the station staff. Fred Arenburg became manager and Orville Pulsifer, Jr. was put in the program director's slot. Since the station was owned at that time by *The Chronicle Herald*, which was, in turn, owned by the Dennis family, Graham Dennis sent down Ron Slade as news director. News was very important in private radio at that time. Now it's a nuisance to be sacrificed to the great profit god.

Mike MacNeil became host of the morning show, *Open Mike*, and it became the first morning talk radio show in Nova Scotia. At ten, Brian Sutcliffe came along with the *Coffee Club*, and at 11:30 Mike (or Tex) MacNeil would come back with a show called *Westernaires*. It featured real country music, not the crap that masquerades as country music today. *Westernaires* wasn't a new show. The first host was Don Tremaine, my friend and mentor. Don was known as "Trigger" Tremaine. The name Trigger stuck with him through his entire career in radio and television. When I hosted *Westernaires* (not very often) I was known as Cactus Cameron. I'm glad that name didn't stick. Brian Sutcliffe ended up in Sydney as a CBC announcer-producer. I hosted a live New Year's Eve show for him sometime during the late '80s.

Afternoons on CHNS were pretty scary. Bob Oxley did early afternoons and then part of the drive show. He later joined me at the CBC. He retired from the Corp about the same time as me and now lives in St. John's, Newfoundland.

Brian Sutcliffe also did a show from three to four in the afternoon. He appealed to the adults and I came along at four with the teenage portion. The show was *You Call the Play* and the premise was: Send us your name and phone number on a postcard and we'll call you and play your request. One young lass used to send out songs for all the guys on the *Bonaventure*, one of three old British aircraft carriers that became part of the Royal Canadian Navy. Anyone who could take on the entire crew of an aircraft carrier had my complete attention.

You Call the Play finished at five, and Bob Oxley (or the Golden Ox, as we called him) rolled you home between five and six. Bob joined the CBC shortly after me, and we both ended up on *Information Morning*, Nova Scotia's news and current affairs program that began in 1970 and is still number one.

I spoke of the importance of news. Well, at six p.m. CHNS went for the news audience with a half-hour program called *News Orbit*. It was the space age, after all. I recall one night *News Orbit* went ten minutes overtime. I would not have had a problem with that except the commercials scheduled between 6:30 and 7:00 had to go because it was triple "A" time: like prime-time TV, advertisers pay more for commercials during peak hours, when they have the biggest audience. The four-to-seven slot was one of these periods. If the ads weren't played before seven, the station couldn't charge the higher rate. After the news I played three commercials back to back, opened my mike and said, "We interrupt these commercials to bring you a record."

I know. I shouldn't have said that. It would piss off our sponsors, but it really pissed off the news editor at the time, Jerry Kendrick. He came flying into the control room, using some colourful language that made his feelings really clear. He became program director after I left CHNS, and gave up the colourful language. He's now a senior pastor at a church in Halifax and station manager of CIRP Life 94.7 FM.

After *You Call the Play* at four, I hosted *The Frank Cameron Show* from 6:30 until 11:00. There was a thirty-minute Bible thumper between 9:30 and 10:00. I had to work harder to get back the audience I lost during this half-hour. During the show, which was on reel-to-reel tape, I used to open the mike and break wind loudly. Not once did we get a call about noises on the tape. I guess the show didn't have much of an audience.

I would stay every night till midnight and do a fifteen-minute newscast that included (by order of the CRTC) the marine weather. Those minutes were the longest of my life. The guys I worked with tried everything in their arsenal to crack me up during those long news and weathercasts. I recall Bob Chisholm and Hal Blackadar rushing into the news booth with an ashtray full of burning toxic material. It was the waste from a disc-cutting machine and the smell would gag a maggot. Other times I'd look up into the control room and see three bare asses and three sets of testicles up against the window. I soldiered on.

I got a call in late 1961 from a young man who was at the newly opened Halifax International Airport. He said his name was Bobby Curtola. He was from Port Arthur (now Thunder Bay), Ontario, and he was passing through Halifax on his way to England. He was promoting a song written by his manager, Basil Hurdon. The song was "Hand In Hand With You," and I started playing it on the air immediately. It became a hit and Bobby has become a lifelong friend. To be fair, a Winnipeg disc jockey also played the song and it became a hit there.

Bobby credits me with putting his career into high gear, but I can't take all the credit. His personality played a big part in his rise to fame. When "Fortune Teller" was released he did a mini tour of Nova Scotia. I accompanied him to Truro where a crowd of screaming girls tried to tear his clothes off. Bobby Curtola to me is the original Canadian Idol. Yes, Paul Anka came along in the mid to late '50s, but he found his fame in the U.S. I

With my long-time friend, Bobby Curtola. (Photo courtesy of Seaside Radio.)

remember while working at CKCL in Truro we received some 45s from Regency Records containing songs by Paul Anka from Ottawa. It wasn't until Anka hooked up with Don Costa in New York that he recorded "Diana" and a bunch more of his own songs and became an international sensation.

Bobby Curtola didn't have to go to the U.S. to make his name. He stayed here in Canada. Not only that, he was the main mover and shaker behind the Canadian content rule in Canadian radio. Canadian artists today owe a great deal to this dynamo named Bobby Curtola. They may not have made the charts if not for that rule and the fact that Canadian musicians are now the best in the world. Any radio station that says it's having trouble putting on Canadian content is living under a very large rock. Please note that Canadian artists of the last forty years have so improved the music business in Canada.

Bobby Curtola placed a number of songs on the charts in the U.S. The most notable was "Fortune Teller." He used to go to Las Vegas where he would spend a number of weeks every year entertaining audiences at one of the big hotels. His Vegas shows got rave reviews from Americans and Canadians alike.

A few years ago, he asked me to come to Liverpool (Nova Scotia) to emcee a show he was doing there. I even performed a song with him. Remember the Everly Brothers' "Bird Dog"? I did the lines "He's a bird," and "He's a dog." Bobby did the rest. He was on key. I was not. When my daughter Seanna was in hospital in 1964 with a spinal problem, Bobby Curtola not only came to the hospital to see her, but brought her a stuffed toy. Seanna cherished that toy and she still has it in her possession. At a recent roast held in my honour in Dartmouth, who showed up? Bobby Curtola. When I spent time in hospital in 2012, I could hear some commotion outside my room and someone singing "Fortune Teller." Who was it? Of course. It was Bobby Curtola. I love the guy.

In 1960 and again in 1961 a song called "The Twist," performed by Ernest Evans (a.k.a. Chubby Checker), came out and a dance craze subsequently followed. It was the only song ever to go to number one two years in a row. Written by Hank Ballard, Chubby made the song a hit. It spawned a whole lot of other dances: the Pony, the Mashed Potato, and the Hucklebuck. The Peppermint Lounge (based on the song "Peppermint Twist") opened on lower Barrington Street in downtown Halifax. It had a house band called Kenny Weeks and the Meteors, and whenever I hear Joey Dee and the Starliters doing "Peppermint Twist," my mind flashes back to the early '60s and the Peppermint Lounge. Kenny Weeks was a wonderful guy. He died in 2009 at age seventy, and some of the band still exists.

I'm often asked to name my favourite song of all time. I wrestle with that one because there are so many from which to choose. If you're talking about doo-wop I have to go with "In the Still of the Night" by the Five Satins. In pop music I have to defer. I don't have a favourite pop song. In country music Garth Brooks turns my crank with "The River," and in rock I'm torn between "A Whiter Shade of Pale" by Procol Harum and "In My Life" by the Beatles. John Lennon's "Imagine" is a great piece of work. The producers of the movie *The Killing Fields* used the Lennon song in a particularly poignant scene of that depressing flick, and I defy you not to shed tears during that part of the movie.

I like all music, even some hip hop. Gangsta Rap is carefully calculated to exploit young people with its potty-mouth language and questionable subject matter. And regular rap is mostly bad poetry and a drum machine. There used to be categories for country music that made the pop charts. They were known as crossovers, but that category no longer exists. It's just music. Period.

My favourite Christmas song is "White Christmas" by Clyde MacPhatter and the Drifters. Now before Bing Crosby fans have a hissy fit, let me explain. Until 1954 the only version of "White Christmas" played on radio was by Bing Crosby. It's a nice version, but it was done to death. When the Drifters' version came out in 1954, most radio stations didn't play it for the same reason they played the white versions of black doo-wop and rhythm and blues songs. And in this case why play a rock version of the song when Bing Crosby was available?

When I worked in Truro in the late '50s, I recall the record librarian showing me a note from the Canadian Association of Broadcasters (CAB) concerning "Mary's Boy Child." I'll paraphrase it. The CAB advises member stations not to play "Mary's Boy Child" by the Voices of Walter Schumann. It has been deemed to be sacrilegious by a number of church groups. Translation: The Christian bullies don't want you to play this song. Yet the Harry Belafonte version was fine. The Voices of Walter Schumann did it in true calypso style. It was uptempo and it was great. It wasn't that Harry didn't do it justice. It turned out the CAB looked stupid and hypocritical and the radio stations followed like sheep.

By 1962 CHNS was basking in the glory of the all-important ratings when a young man from Prince Edward Island arrived. His name was Mike Duffy, and he started at CHNS by doing the late news shift. Mike had a nose for news and we became pretty good buddies. He left CHNS before I did, and we eventually ended up at the CBC together.

In the fall of 1962 CHNS was broadcasting live from the Maritime Winter Fair at the Halifax Forum grounds. Riding the wave of the space age, the station commissioned a company to build a replica of a spaceship and hired a crane to lift this thing high into the air. You should have seen that bird lifting this heavy object. Just kidding. But we were broadcasting from a spaceship.

One afternoon, the crane operator let me down to earth where I met Orv Pulsifer. He motioned for me to sit in the station vehicle with him. Orv was never one to mince words, so he came right out with it. "Frank," he said (for that was my name), "the ratings just came in." The ratings were, are, and forever shall be the radio station bible. With high ratings come advertising dollars. He went on to say that CHNS had doubled and tripled the ratings, and we now controlled 65 percent of the available radio audience in the Halifax market. He handed me an envelope. Inside was a cheque for a very large sum of money. Seems the Board of Directors at the *Herald* wanted to share the wealth.

CHNS managed to keep that audience for the next seven years. CJCH threw everything at us but the kitchen sink. But to no avail. Keep in mind that AM radio ruled the airwaves at that time. CHNS had an FM station then, but it just re-broadcast the AM signal. In the early '70s AM and FM parted company and CHNS FM became CHFX.

In 1963 the YMCA sponsored a trip to New York over the Easter week. My wife and the mother of our children, Diane, and I hopped aboard the Italian liner *Vulcania* and sailed for New York. Well, almost. We spent the first night on board looking at Pier 21 when the crew went on a twenty-four-hour strike. CHNS was asked to send over some gear so we could do a dance, but the *Vulcania* had DC power and we didn't have converters. Finally, we set sail for the Big Apple.

I was sick of the ten-course meals and the German beer on tap in the First Class bar, so we were happy to get into the third-class hotel in New York. I forget how many teens we had under our wings, but two of them didn't make it to the hotel. They were whisked to the airport and sent home after being caught in the immigrants' bar aboard ship tipping their underage elbows while consuming strong drink. Jon Goldberg, now a Halifax lawyer, was one of them. I remember Jon because he's taller than anyone I know.

The United Nations was boring, but the nights were great. We ate at a swanky Oriental restaurant and attended the big show at Radio City Music Hall. In the lobby of that great New York institution I saw colour TV for the first time. We saw a first-run movie, *Bye Bye Birdie* with Paul Lynde and Bobby Rydell. The famous Rockettes strutted their stuff, and we got to see some puppets known as The Muppets. The next night we went to a Broadway Theatre and saw *Stop the World, I Want to Get Off* with Anthony Newley. Broadway lived up to its reputation and it prompted me to attend our own Neptune Theatre every chance I could.

I was working during the afternoon of Friday, November 22, 1963. It was the day after my twenty-fifth birthday. I was preparing for *You Call the Play* when someone yelled in the newsroom: "Kennedy's been shot!" The Kennedy was John Fitzgerald Kennedy and a terse message had appeared on the United Press International newswire that I paraphrase: "Shots fired at Kennedy motorcade in Dallas ... More to follow."

I was not an American, but I loved Jack Kennedy. He stiffed Nikita Khruschev on the Cuban Missile Crisis and he began to make southern Americans realize how racist they were. He had two small children and the White House was known as Camelot. Yes, he was a womanizer and he came from a rich family, but we all loved him. When I saw the TV images, I cried unashamedly. Who would do this? It was then that I began to realize we have lots to learn about keeping ourselves secure when there are those who would do us harm. For the entire weekend CHNS played sombre music and joined the CBS radio network. That wouldn't happen today. Even then, I thought it was a bit much.

5

1964: Of Frank's Bandstand, Beatles, and Other Happenings

1964 was probably the best year of my life. CHNS and Hatfield Potato Chips sponsored a contest that allowed us to take twenty teens to Toronto to see the Beatles, even though I said the mop tops would never make it. Do I regret that? Damn right I do. The Beatles' first Canadian release came out in October 1963. It was a mediocre song, "From Me To You." Since they already had three number one hits in Britain I should have picked up on it. But I didn't and neither did Capitol Records, U.S.A. They farmed out the Beatles to little labels such as VeeJay and Tollie Records, but when "I Want To Hold Your Hand" hit the North American airwaves in January 1964, they changed their tune. So did I.

When it was announced publicly that I was going to host a TV show on the CBC, some members of the board of directors at *The Chronicle Herald* weren't too

The weekly CHNS Top 60 chart advertising the Beatles contest trip.

happy. I was told by CHNS management there was concern in the big-shot ranks about me making all that extra money. The problem seemed to be that if I worked on contract for the CBC, all the other announcers would want to do the same thing. My reply to the Board of Directors was (with respect) kiss my red rosy butt. If any of the other CHNS personalities were given the opportunity to do a TV show, you're damn right they'd do it.

Anyway, here we were on an Air Canada Vanguard on Labour Day weekend, 1964, headed for Tranna. Once again Diane and I became chaperones. We were accompanied by Orv Pulsifer and his wonderful wife, Ruth. We took a side trip to Niagara Falls. For most of us, it was our first time at the Falls. Then it was back to

960's SUPER 60

CHNS Chart for Week of August 9th to 15th, 1964

TW	LW	Title / Artist
1	2	**If I Fell and I Love Her** Beatles
2	14	**Where Did Our Love Go** The Supremes
3	3	**Ain't She Sweet** Beatles
4	5	**Little Old Lady** Jan & Dean
5	1	**Hard Days Night** Beatles
6	6	**She's My Girl** Bobby Shafto
7	9	**Under the Boardwalk** The Drifters
8	4	**Rag Doll** Four Seasons
9	11	**It Hurts To Be In Love** Gene Pitney
10	10	**Tell Me** Rolling Stones
11	13	**Do I Love You** Ronettes
12	19	**People Say** Dixiecups
13	7	**Wishin' & Hopin'** Dusty Springfield
14	9	**You're My World** Cilla Black
15	12	**Nobody I Know** Peter & Gordon
15	15	**She's The One** Chartbusters
16	17	**A Million Drums** Jimmy Clanton
17	18	**Someone Someone** Brian Poole
18	22	**Handy Man** Del Shannon
19	21	**Hey Harmonica Man** Stevie Wonder
20	16	**Memphis** Johnny Rivers
21	23	**Everybody Loves** Dean Martin
22	26	**Lookin' For Boys** Pin Ups
23	24	**Muddah Faddah, 1964** Allan Sherman
24	—	**Sweet William*** Millie Small
25	27	**I Never Dreamed** Cookies
26	34	**Little Latin Lupe Lu** Kingsmen
27	41	**Because** Dave Clark Five
28	50	**I Want You To Meet** Eydie Gorme
29	29	**Here I Go Again** Hollies
30	30	**Like Dreamers Do** Applejacks
31	35	**Al Di La** Ray Charles Singers
32	37	**I Wanna Love Him** Jelly Beans
33	55	**You Never Can Tell** Chuck Berry
34	38	**Maybe I Know** Lesley Gore
35	39	**Looking For Love** Connie Francis
36	43	**I Will** Billy Fury
37	45	**A Tear Fell** Ray Charles
38	48	**Walk Don't Run '64** Ventures
39	36	**Jimmy Johnny or Joe** Lynda Lane
40	25	**C'mon Everybody** Elvis Presley
41	29	**I Get Around** Beach Boys
42	31	**Can't You See That** Dave Clark Five
43	40	**Johnny Loves Me** Florraine Darlin
43	44	**In My Imagination** Paul Anka
44	60	**It's All Over Now** Rolling Stones
45	57	**Should I Cry** Concords
46	46	**Sailor Boy** Chiffons
47	47	**Hangin' Onto My** Tracey Dey
48	56	**Never Pick A** Dee Dee Sharp
49	59	**Someday We're Gonna Love Again** Searchers
50	58	**You're No Good** Swinging Blue Jeans
51	—	**Come Home Little Girl** Bobby Curtola
52	33	**Sie Leib Dich** Beatles
53	—	**Little Honda** Beach Boys
54	—	**When You Loved Me** Brenda Lee
55	32	**As Long As I'm Sure** Bobby Curtola
56	53	**Worry** Johnny Tillotson
57	—	**Darlin'** Paul & Paula
58	49	**Constantly** Cliff Richard
59	—	**Mary Oh Mary** Fats Domino
60	—	**What Kinda Love** Jimmy Gilmer

CHNS PICK TO CLICK!

CLINGING VINE — Bobby Vinton

*Record that made the biggest jump this week.

The flip side of the Beatles Holiday contest. The Super 60 chart for August 9-15, 1964. The Beatles held down numbers 1, 3, 5, and 52. Bobby Curtola appears twice, at #51 ("Come Home Little Girl") and #55 ("As Long As I'm Sure").

Toronto where I attended a bizarre press conference with the Beatles at Maple Leaf Gardens. All four were in top form as they faced the questions from the press. Their answers were hilarious. Ashtrays were brought out for the group and a Toronto newspaper reporter noted that John Lennon smoked the whole time. She rose and said, "Mr. Lennon, you have been smoking through this entire press conference. Don't you think you're setting a bad example for our young people?" Before she could sit down, Ringo Starr reached under the table, brought out a bottle of booze, and said, "And he drinks, too!"

I say the conference was bizarre because the newspaper reporters wouldn't let anyone but themselves ask questions. Back then they were press conferences. Today they would be news conferences. I don't remember much about it because the questions from the newspaper reporters were too long and boring. It was difficult for TV reporters to get a word in, and the whole session lasted only a few minutes. I wish I had a transcript of that event, but I couldn't lay my hands on one. All I remember is, the printed press in those days made a mockery of rock and roll performers and at this particular conference they had met their match. You ask dumb questions. You get smart answers. It's as simple as that.

The eight p.m. concert at Maple Leaf Gardens was, like the press conference, bizarre. The warm-up acts included an American group called the Exciters. They did the original recording of "Do-Wah-Diddy" a year before South Africa's Manfred Mann. One of the singers was eight months pregnant, but they were fun. Along came Gene Simmons (no, not *that* Gene Simmons), who did a song called "Haunted House." Clarence Frogman Henry was also on the bill. The Bill Black combo performed, and a personal favourite of mine, Jackie DeShannon, who wrote much of her own material.

Then came the Beatles. The screams were bloodcurdling. The only time the noise abated was when Paul McCartney spoke. You could hear a pin drop. I think it was his British accent that turned those female heads. He didn't say much. But then, he didn't have to. He could have recited bad poetry and no one would have cared. But rap music didn't show up until the '80s (cheap shot). After an hour of this madness the Beatles were gone. The lights came on and the St. John Ambulance moved in. A number of young girls sat bleeding profusely where they had ripped their arms to shreds. I had never been exposed to that kind of frenzy. It ceased to exist with the invention of the cellphone and other such devices that young people have embraced like the plague. Nowadays if you want a Beatles song you just go to YouTube.

Early in 1964 I got a call from Manny Pittson, who was producing *Singalong Jubilee*, a summer replacement for *The Don Messer Show* on CBC. He invited me to come and audition for a new show the CBC was planning. It was called *Music Hop* and was Canada's incarnation of the very popular *American Bandstand*. The Halifax version would be one of five across Canada and would have in-studio dancers.

I hadn't been on television before, so I said sure, I'll do the audition. I showed up at the Bell Road studios one Saturday afternoon. I already had the job, but I went through the motions and pretty soon we started rehearsals for *Frank's Bandstand*. We had a superb cast including bandleader Brian Ahern, who later married the American country singer Emmylou Harris and produced albums for artists including Harris, Anne Murray, Linda Ronstadt, and Johnny Cash. Our drummer was Jack Lilly, who later married Karen Oxley, one of our vocalists. Jimmy White played guitar and Ritchie Oakley was on bass. We had a succession of piano players with vocalist Patrician Anne MacKinnon (also known as Patricia or Trish, who also had a relationship with Brian Ahern) and an African Canadian named D.J. Jeffries. Many of these folks also appeared on *Singalong Jubilee*.

Our audio resources included Bob Theakston and Marty Raine. Our studio production assistant was Athan Katsos and in the control room beside Manny Pittson was a woman I still know and love, Penny Longley. Penny had a poodle named Duffy and he became the show's mascot. D.J. Jeffries lasted one season with us. Along

With an old poster advertising ***Frank's Bandstand***.

came Davey Welles (real name David Upshaw), who could sing anything. He was an amazing guy.

In 1965 Manny decided to experiment a little by taking the show outside. We shot scenes in Point Pleasant Park and the Public Gardens and other places. I remember Patricia (Trish) singing the old folk song "The Cruel War" beside one of the old cannons in Point Pleasant Park. This, to me, was the beginning of the music video, and Manny was the mover and shaker behind it.

I remember donning an old long coat and wearing dark makeup for a segment we called Keeper of the Crypt. I would rise from a crypt in a graveyard (studio, actually) with a knife sticking out of my back, wearing a top hat and doing the worst Bela Lugosi impression you've ever heard. I introduced an older song and thus we get the crypt analogy. Karen Oxley used to dress in a Raggedy Ann costume with pigtails and talk to me about the "oldie" we were about to introduce. Sometimes we'd hang around and dance to the music with the dancers. Karen said it looked like a rag doll dancing with Ebenezer Scrooge.

In the studio we hired a group of dancers to appear on the show, recruited from various high schools, and many were African Nova Scotians. That brought the racists out of the woodwork. We got many calls from the Halifax area decrying the fact that there weren't enough lily white kids on the show. We ignored the bigots and had the best show in the country.

The Montreal version (*Jeunesse Oblige*) I barely remember, but the Toronto show featured DJ Dave Mickie and some very talented Toronto musicians. In Winnipeg the program was known as *Hootenanny* and featured an aboriginal singer and host, Ray St. Germain. The Vancouver show was known as *Let's Go*. Hosted by Red Robinson and Terry David Mulligan, it featured a young woman named Susan Pesklevits, who later married Terry Jacks and formed the Poppy Family. And back in Winnipeg *Music Hop* was taken over by a rock group known as Chad Allan and the Expressions, later to become Guess Who. Burton Cummings and Randy Bachman started their careers on the CBC.

Manny Pittson taught me more about television than anyone else. I remember one day in 1966 we were hanging out in the studio while the technicians were putting Karen Oxley's voice on a pre-recorded band track. The song was the Patti Page hit "Hush, Hush, Sweet Charlotte," and Karen was singing her little heart out as Bob Theakston was playing the track and adding her voice. She had the only live mike in the studio at the time, but soon she was joined by a group of amateurs in the background singing "Flush, Flush the Toilet." The studio door burst open and there was Manny screaming at the top of his voice. "Later for the peanut gallery!" he shouted. I had never seen him lose his temper before. He was a pro, and I loved him dearly. Manny died in 2013.

Frank's Bandstand was on the air from 1964 to 1968 on the CBC TV network. Manny left in 1966, to be replaced by Paul Baylis. I had great fun with Paul. After *Music Hop*, he produced a live noon-hour show called *Roundabout* from the Hotel Nova Scotian five days a week. I hosted the show and we featured mostly public service interviews and music.

Roundabout was responsible for exposing a lot of local talent, particularly the folk music field. Betty Belmore comes to mind. Betty not only sang, but she later did part-time makeup work for the CBC. She is still singing to this day. Another product of *Roundabout* was Kevin MacMichael, who appeared regularly on the show. He eventually went to London and helped form the band Cutting Crew. Kevin and Nick Van Eede had a big hit in 1986 with "I Just Died in Your Arms Tonight." After Cutting Crew, Kevin spent some time with Robert Plant. He came home in the late '90s, but we lost him on New Year's Eve 2002. We lost producer Paul Baylis in 2011. He died at his home on P.E.I.

The story is told about my friend Wayne Adams and his escapades while working at CHNS. Wayne hosted a program directed at the African Nova Scotian community and his programs were informative and entertaining. One day one of the CHNS program hosts began to talk about Aunt Jemima, and what started as an innocent tribute to pancake mix came out as a mild racial slur. Wayne Adams seized the opportunity to have some fun. He quickly ran down the hall of the old

CHNS building, flung open the door to master control, and presented himself as a seething black mass about to strike. The offender, unaware that Wayne was having him on, jumped out the window of the master control room, landing in the bushes below. He had no broken bones, and was terrified until Wayne caught up to him and told him he was only going to give him a mild lecture on racism and how it works.

The story has become a legend, and I remember telling it at a roast we held for Dr. Adams. Wayne sat for six terms on Halifax City Council beginning in 1979, and was elected to the Nova Scotia Legislature in 1993 where he stayed until 1998. During part of that time he was Minister of the Environment and was responsible for introducing Nova Scotia's recycling program, which is light-years ahead of many other jurisdictions. I am proud to call him my friend.

I left CHNS in 1967 and became a full-time employee of the CBC in the spring of that year. It was just in time for Expo 67, the Montreal World's Fair that helped Canada celebrate its 100th anniversary.

6

CBC: A Cast of Characters

In 1967 I hosted music shows on CBC Radio, including classical music programs, morning shows, and everything in between. The elitists were running the place at the time, and they looked down their noses at this rock and roll DJ who infringed on their territory. I remember the first newscast I read on CBC Radio. It was at one o'clock in the afternoon and it ran for fifteen minutes. My performance (pardon my ego) was flawless. I came out hoping to confront those hoity-toity language police, but they had all crawled into the woodwork. One of my supporters was Doug Fraser, who was a fan to begin with. He was senior editor in the radio newsroom at the time. Doug was a really interesting guy who believed in me as a broadcaster. I appreciated that. He was a dear friend.

Frank's Bandstand lasted until 1968, after which I became an all-around staff announcer. I did both radio and television and spent many days and nights in the "booth." Your assignment in the booth was to do commercials and intros and station breaks in between programs. One night, I was feeling a bit bored. Just before the station break on TV there was a commercial for the perfume, Chanel No. 5. At the end of the spot, sexy Catherine Deneuve looked into the camera and said, "Every girl alive loves Chanel No. 5." On came the slide with CBHT on it and I said in the five-second voiceover (in my best French accent), "But for you and me it's Chanel No. 3, CBHT." I thought I would catch it for that, but I never heard a word.

Whenever I was assigned to the booth on Thursday nights, I used to do an intro for what was called *Adventure Theatre*. More often than not, the movie was a horror flick and I did the intro in what I like to think was a fair Bela Lugosi impression. One night the movie was *It Came From Outer Space*. It was about a giant spore that attacked the earth. I said it was subtitled There's A Fungus Amungus. As I said, I was bored in the booth.

Speaking of commercials, Coca-Cola always had the best TV commercials. The ad agency looking after Coke's commercials has always contained some very imaginative individuals. In 1971 the agency produced the famous Hillside spot, which shows a number of young people of different nationalities singing a jingle which went something like this: "I'd like to teach the world to sing in perfect harmony. I'd like to buy the world a Coke and keep it company." It was a testimonial to diversity in the U.S. and it soon went into commercial production as a hit song. The Coke references were removed and the Hillside Singers and the New Seekers made it into a chart song.

In 2014, the folks at Coca-Cola produced a new commercial. It was a version of "America the Beautiful," a wonderful patriotic song written by an American

English professor in 1895. It was sung in five different languages, including English and Spanish and even Arabic. It was once again a tribute to diversity, but the bigots at Fox News and the regular bigots who populate the social media were all over it. "Speak English or get out of the country!" they cried. Keep in mind these are the people who inhabit the Internet and spew hate daily. They suffer from eye strain and a lack of vitamin D. And they're not just Americans. Every country, including Canada, is full of them.

In June 1970, the fuddy-duddy CBC set Halifax on its ear by introducing morning talk radio. The show was *Information Morning*, a series of interviews sandwiched in between the latest news, weather, and sports. The first host was Bob Oxley. He was the chief interviewer and the traffic cop and he was joined by co-host Paul Kells and two ... count 'em ... two newscasters. One was Brian Bulloch, who was replaced by Doug Arnold. George Young handled the sports and Reid Dexter, a real meteorologist, presented the weather. When Canada joined the rest of the world (with one big exception) on the metric system in the early '70s, Reid rejoiced. The Canadian weather service, now known as Environment Canada, had to convert all the temperatures and wind speeds from other countries into the old imperial system. Not anymore. Celsius and kilometres ruled. Reid used to say, "It's 20 degrees Celsius. That's 68 foolish." The foolish stood for Fahrenheit.

One bright morning Doug and I were reading the news when he began an item thusly: "Three male students at St. F.X. University have been suspended for entering girls in their room. That should read entertaining girls in their room." The studio erupted into giggles and laughter that could probably be heard out on Sackville Street. The feminists and politically correct producers

With my mentor and friend Don Tremaine and kids at the IWK Children's Hospital in 1986 or 1987. CBC-TV hosted the IWK Telethon from 1984 to 1994.

tried to cover it up, but the horse was out of the barn. George Young left his seat at the table, went to a corner of the studio, and assumed the crouching position. The technician cut the mikes and replayed an Oland's beer commercial that had just aired a few minutes before.

Information Morning was later hosted by my friend and mentor Don Tremaine, until he retired in the early '90s, when the present host, Don Connolly, took over. The show remains number one in the Halifax morning market to this day, much to the chagrin of the other radio stations. It's now appealing to a fourth generation and shows no signs of slowing down.

Let me say a few words about the two Dons. Of all the many good role models I've had, Don Tremaine really taught me how to be a broadcaster, but he was never overbearing in his instruction. Any corrections were always done very gently and with humour. Case in point: Like my father Harvey, he was a stickler for the English language. When I first encountered the word "dysentery" on the page and mispronounced it, he did give me the proper pronunciation but added, "You've probably heard it, but never seen it written down."

One year I delivered a Christmas message from Syd Kennedy, regional director for the Maritimes, and right there on-air blanked out on Syd's position. Tremaine leaned over, without any fanfare, and said into the mike, "That's the regional director." Don's the most professional broadcaster I've ever met – he can do all the things a pro should be able to do: ad lib, read well, pass on knowledge to up-and-comers, have a good rapport with peers. It's a given that media personalities have an ego – you can't do the job without it – but Tremaine taught me how to control mine, how to handle rudeness and how to be knowledgeable but not put people off. And while many colleagues tried to crack me up on-air, you simply couldn't throw Tremaine. Like I said, professional to the bone.

Don Connolly, who I call "the Communist from Bathurst" because of his slightly left-wing views, worked in private radio before joining CBC. All of the *Information Morning* hosts were and are good interviewers, but Don's one of the best, quick on the uptake and he knows what buttons to push. He's a good friend.

My big entrance into TV came in 1964 with *Frank's Bandstand*, but I went daily in the early '70s when I took on the task of presenting the seven p.m. evening news, which followed *Gazette*, the six o'clock current affairs show. Before I get into the supper-hour show, a bit of history.

CBHT came on the air in late 1954. It carried programs on film (no microwave yet) and *Gazette*, a local show hosted by Don Tremaine and Max Ferguson. The weather was handled by Rube Hornstein. Rube knew more about the weather than any ten of today's meteorologists. He used a big blackboard and chalk to present the forecast. Since the show was live, any glitch could be covered. When a guest didn't show up, Don or Max would say, "Rube, let's talk about troughs." And they would. For five or six minutes.

Max Ferguson came from CBC radio where he was known as Rawhide. Max had a cast of characters on his radio show of the same name. Rawhide played country music (which Max hated) and did an impersonation of a CBC announcer whom he called Marvin Mellowbell. He also wrote three books, beginning with *And Now Here's Max*, the title being based on Allan McFee's introduction to *The Max Ferguson Show* (which had various incarnations: 1962-1973, 1973-1998).

One Christmas Eve Max brought his bulldog into the studio. As the dog slept under the Christmas tree, Max, Rube, and Don sat around the phony fireplace and reminisced about Christmases past. The dog didn't much like uniforms, so when Santa showed up with his ho ho ho and his belly heaving like a bowl full of jelly, the dog took exception. He chased Santa out the door, biting his butt and snorting in a low-pitched growl. The story is told by Max in one of his books, but I happened to be watching that night. It was hilarious. That's why the audience loved *Gazette*. There was the debonair Tremaine with the news, the knowledgeable Rube with the weather, and the unpredictable Max with the comic relief.

Sports in those days were handled by the intrepid Pat Connolly, who knew more about the subject than anyone I've ever known. If you challenged Pat with a trivia sports contest, you did it at your peril. Pat and I were friends for more than forty years when he died in 2012. He was a warm, kind, loving guy, and he is much missed.

One night I was watching CBC sports and the funniest thing happened. The intro and extro (TV terms) for the sports consisted of a turning pedestal with a statuette surrounded by hanging pieces of crepe paper. At the end of the sportscast, the pedestal came on screen and CBC sports was superimposed (another TV term) on a slide. Suddenly, the whole shooting match (not a TV term) was picked up and set aside by a stagehand. Live.

Gazette hosted the famous "chowder party" in the late '60s. A challenge was issued to find out who made the best seafood chowder. I was working in the booth that night, so I had a clear view of the whole thing. Syd Kennedy, the regional director, was in the studio along with then program director Paddy Gregg and some chowder was being made, live, on air. The guys were into their "cups" that night and I can still remember Paddy talking about his chowder recipe while standing behind the cauldron. He was smoking a cigarette (yes, you could smoke on air then) and since his hands were busy, he had to stick the lit cigarette in his mouth. A very long ash was dangling over the chowder pot and, sure enough, it dropped into the chowder. Paddy didn't see it fall, but he didn't miss a beat. It looked like a scene out of *Monty Python's Flying Circus*. It was some of the funniest television I ever witnessed.

Shortly after that incident, I joined the cast of *Gazette*. Don Tremaine and Rube Hornstein alternated on interviews, while I did the news and the odd interview. Speaking of odd interviews, I was given the task of interviewing *Chatelaine* magazine's Mother of

On ***Gazette*** in 1979. Standing: Ron Hill, Marilyn MacDonald, Pat Connolly, Reid Dexter. Seated: Rube Hornstein, Don Tremaine, and me.

the Year. I'm the first to admit that my interview skills weren't the best (still aren't), but I thought, This is going to be a breeze. In the makeup room the woman was bubbly and animated, so I figured, No problem.

When the show went to air, it became a problem. I asked the standard questions we were taught in the CBC training department. "How does it feel to be Mother of the Year?"

"Fine" was the reply. No elaboration.

Okay, let's move on.

"How does your family feel about it?"

"Fine."

"What does your husband think of it?"

"Fine."

The fact is, the poor woman choked, and there was little I could do about it. The interview was scheduled for five minutes and it lasted two. I could hear Charlie Reynolds, the director in the control room, screaming in his Irish brogue, "What's he doing? The goddamn interview is supposed to go five minutes!" I doubt if anyone could have saved this interview.

The best interview I ever did (if I may be so bold) was on radio. I was hosting *Mainstreet* on CBC Radio one fine afternoon and the producer said, "Have I got a gem for you." The gem turned out to be June Callwood, a woman I had admired from afar for many years. June was a jourmalist and political activist during her career at *The Globe and Mail* and then as a freelancer. She was a staunch advocate of the rights of women and children and she started a hospice for AIDS victims in the dark days of the epidemic. The interview concerned her new book, *Jim: A Life With AIDS*. I was so engrossed in the interview, we used up all the time allotted and then some. The producer of the program just let it go. I felt so comfortable interviewing this woman that the questions kept coming and the answers followed with ease. June Callwood made it easy, because she was so comfortable behind a microphone.

She died of cancer in 2007 and I mourned her loss along with thousands of Canadians. She had written a dozen books and her articles in *Mclean's Magazine* and other publications were read by millions. Her TV appearances were many. Her last appearance on CBC Television was on April 2, 2007, when she was interviewed by George Stroumboulopoulos, and I think I know how George felt while talking to this great woman. June Callwood died less than two weeks after this interview.

As *Gazette* morphed from a nice local current affairs show into a hard-nosed news and current affairs show, a parade of hosts and interviewers went through the Bell Road building like a flight of Canada geese.

Rex Murphy, who still does commentary for the network and is a hell of a writer, came to Halifax from Newfoundland to do interviews for *Here Today* or whatever incarnation *Gazette* was at the time. I remember Rex taking on Greenpeace on the seal hunt. He totally humiliated one of the protesters.

Rex has a genius I.Q. and had some on-again off-again problems, but he seems to have everything under control and hosts a weekly call-in show on CBC Radio called *Cross Country Checkup*. To hear him on television, you'd never think he was a climate change denier or an oil pipeline advocate, but he is. In his home province of Newfoundland he referred to Premier Joey Smallwood as a dictator, and he ran for both the Tories and the Liberals in provincial elections. He spent some time working for Clyde Wells when Clyde was the Liberal premier of Newfoundland. If Rex Murphy decided to run for prime minister of Canada, I wouldn't care which party he was with – I'd vote for him.

In the late 1970s, Sharon Dunn arrived from Sydney where she had been presenting the weather on CJCB TV. I had a brief fling with Sharon. Since I wasn't living with my wife at that time, it was not an "affair." Sharon was a looker and every horny male in Halifax with a BMW constantly harassed her. I remember one night having dinner with her at a downtown Halifax restaurant when this guy approached our table and said, "Aren't you Sharon Dunn?" "Yes," was the reply and I'll paraphrase what this guy said: "I've got my BMW idling outside the restaurant and I'll take you anywhere you want to go, like my place."

I didn't have to say a word. Sharon went up one side of this guy and down the other, pointing out to the idiot that she was having dinner and he was an interruptor. He left with his tail between his legs. The first time Sharon did an interview on the supper-hour program, we got a couple of calls from some macho jocks saying women shouldn't be on television. Sharon was devastated, but I told her to grow a pair and I think she listened to me. She now lives in Toronto.

Leslie MacKinnon spent some time in Halifax as a co-host for the suppertime news. She is now a senior correspondent for the CBC in Ottawa. Leslie didn't see eye to eye with the pragmatic Rube Hornstein, and she used to think up little things when she introduced him with the weather. I recall one night she said to Rube, "Is this rain ever going to end?" to which Rube replied, "Well, it always has before." Zing!

In the mid '80s, a young man came to work for the summer at CBC Halifax. He was attending law school at Dalhousie University, but he arrived with a radio pedigree. Ian Hanomansing had paid his dues working in radio in Amherst and Moncton and at my old alma mater, CHNS. While he was in his final year in law school, I was privileged to be one of the judges of a public speaking championship at Mount Saint Vincent University in Halifax, where contestants had to deliver a five-minute talk on a topic given right then. Ian won hands down. He began to fill in for me as an anchor on the supper-hour show. He spent some time as a national reporter for CBC Maritimes, and soon he was off to Toronto. After a stint there, he went to Vancouver where he remains to this day as anchor for the News Network.

Here's some irony. (Stay with me – I'll get to it.) When the earthquake devastated Haiti in 2010, my granddaughter Sage (Seanna's daughter) had just arrived in Port-au-Prince with her grade twelve class from Mount Sentinel Secondary in South Slocan, British Columbia. The students were going to live on a farm just outside the capital. Many of the kids were from farming backgrounds and were going to pass on their knowledge of goat-raising to the Haitian farmer, who was growing crops. The trip was also a public relations thing – greetings from Canada and such.

Sage was brushing her hair when the mirror on the wall started to move. The quake scared the hell out of the kids, and they spent some time stranded in the countryside, sleeping on the ground because their accommodation at the Grand Goave compound was badly damaged. As well, they had a considerable sum of money stolen. But, being resilient youngsters, they took the bull by the horns (metaphorically speaking) and pooled their remaining money to buy a huge bag of rice to feed the folks on the farm for a few days.

Sage and her friends grew up during this period. They saw things that seventeen-year-olds should not be seeing. The estimated death toll is 230,000, and the area was dangerous not only because of possible aftershocks but due to the ensuing lawlessness that made being there unsafe and life uncertain.

When Seanna called me she was frantic with worry. I called Jamie Lipsit, the CBC Halifax assignment editor, who told me, "Give me half an hour." When Jamie phoned back, he said the assignment editor in Toronto had contacted Susan Ormiston, who was in Haiti covering the earthquake story, and told her about the stranded Canadian students. Susan went to the Canadian Embassy, wangled a bus (with something like "These are our kids and we've got to help them"), and headed to the little farming town to pick up the high school students.

There were two Canadian soldiers on board the bus, and they escorted them to the embassy, telling the kids to keep their heads down. They were upfront with them: there might be shooting. After a day at the embassy waiting for transport out of the country, Sage and her friends boarded a Canadian Forces plane that flew them to Montreal. WestJet flew them from there back to Nelson, B.C. One of the young Haitians gave Sage his prized possession as a gift: a machete in its sheath. She got it into Canada; officials didn't give her any problem.

I did a cut-in interview from Halifax with Newsworld. The anchor interviewed me with a picture of my red-haired granddaughter over my shoulder. Sage later told her mother she wanted to go back to Haiti, that she had left under protest. "These people have nothing." She was troubled by the inequality, why some people have so much and others so little. As I say, these kids grew up because of this experience.

One year after the earthquake, the CBC in Vancouver thought they would revisit the high school students (now graduated) and talk about their experiences one year later. Who was assigned to do the interview? Ian Hanomansing. He actually gave Sage a lift home. When she told him who her grandfather was, he almost went off the road. Small world.

Gerry Regan was doing play by play at CJCH when I worked at CKCL in Truro. He went on to become premier of Nova Scotia. His son Geoff is an MP and his daughter-in-law Kelly is an MLA. His daughter Nancy worked at CTV for a long time and now does freelance television. His youngest daughter Laura is an accomplished actress who has appeared in a number of movies, most notably the TV movie *Saving Jessica Lynch* and a goodly number of TV shows including *Heartland, Law and Order, CSI Miami*, and a half-dozen episodes of the Emmy award winner *Mad Men*.

Ken Bagnell appeared one season on *Here Today*. I hadn't been in touch since he became Reverend and was editing the *United Church Observer*. Even though he had gone to the printed word, I guess he couldn't get the spoken word out of his system (no pun intended). I tried to contact Ken to get a comment for this book, but I might as well have tried to get through to the Kremlin.

Steve Armitage is a Dartmouth boy who presented the sports on the supper-hour show for a number of years. He's still with the CBC in Vancouver. Marilyn MacDonald was a host interviewer during that period, and her introductions of Steve were funny and wonderful. Marilyn was a bright light on the show. Her interviews were well researched and I admired her for her great sense of humour. She was up there with the best of them. She went to Dalhousie University after leaving the CBC and is still the big dog in the university's communications department.

Colleen Jones was a CBC steal from ATV, later CTV. I remember meeting Colleen at a social function while she was working for ATV. She asked me what was going on at CBC and did I think she had a chance of joining the Corporation. I said yes. Don't get me wrong. I had nothing to do with her getting the job. The CBC was impressed by her eagerness and talent. They hired her and she's still there. Colleen has covered the Olympics and many other major sporting events for the CBC. She covers major curling events, except when she's competing in them. She's a champion curler.

1st Edition: me, Colleen Jones, Jim Nunn, and Norma Lee MacLeod.

Susan Ormiston, who I mentioned earlier, became a reporter at CBC Halifax and was a co-anchor on the supper-hour news during the early '80s. At that time, she was just getting her feet wet as an anchor. She's very good at it, but she prefers reporting and is now one of the CBC's senior correspondents. She did some stuff for CTV in the '90s, but came home in 2001. She is based in Toronto but reports from all over the world.

Norma Lee MacLeod was a fresh face from Prince Edward Island in the '80s. She hosted the show with Jim Nunn and I was your friendly non-meteorologist weather forecaster. Jim was a pretty serious fellow and Norma Lee was serious when the situation warranted, but could hold her own in any situation.

I was one hip guy in these plaid pants.

When CBC got its first satellite truck, we did the weather from some of the weirdest places, including Citadel Hill. One evening, while I was tripping and skipping up Citadel Hill with my trusty CBC umbrella, a thunder cell went over and I thought: Great. Lightning always goes for higher ground. The wind came up, blew my umbrella inside out. I got soaked and seconds before we went on the air, the cameraman yelled, "One more like that and I'm out of here!" I cleaned that up for public consumption. There I was on camera, soaked to the skin, my umbrella turned inside out, trying to do the weather. The crew cracked up, including the dour Jim Nunn. Norma Lee maintained her composure, barely.

I had provided the evening's entertainment, and I was happy to do it. When I finished the weather bit, I zipped home so I could get out of the wet clothes, and didn't make it back in time to do the last weather hit from the studio. As I told the producer, a person can only do so much for their craft. Norma Lee is currently hosting *Maritime Noon* on CBC Radio, and I think she's found her niche. She was great on television but has built up a big following on radio.

Linda Kelly was a graduate of the University of King's College School of Journalism and arrived at the CBC as a reporter. Soon she was anchoring the supper-hour show. She had a great rapport with me and the other on-air crew, but the producers and technicians loved her as well. Linda now lives in Toronto. She's married to a big-shot insurance guy.

Jim Nunn had a reputation as a tough journalist when he joined the CBC in 1979. He worked in Edmonton, Halifax, and St. John's and returned to Halifax in 1981, where he was soon hosting the supper-hour news.

The CBC wanted a hard-hitting host and I wasn't it. I went from hosting to doing stories and then the weather. I had some problems at that time even to the point of having panic attacks. Committee managers and announcers were apprising staff that you had to be a journalist to have credibility. When you're in the media, your ego is part of your makeup and when it gets kicked in the teeth, it hurts. Then, once I realized I was just what one journalist-turned-manager, referring to booth announcers and script readers, called "a golden throated relic of a bygone era," everything was okay. And I couldn't be hard-hitting because I didn't take myself too seriously.

Jim, on the other hand, had a reputation to fulfill. He got kicked out of St. F.X. University for advocating students' rights, including (among other things) the right to drink on campus. Jim was part of the hippie movement and I recall the two of us sitting in Studio Two on Bell Road waiting to go on the air, singing all four verses of "Sam Stone" by John Prine. Norma Lee thought we were nuts. She never got to hear the song in the proper key.

Having said all that, I like Jim. He was like a bulldog with his interviews, and he was the uncompromising interviewer the CBC was looking for. Or so I thought. The CBC dumped him in 2010. The only reason I can figure is that he was rubbing too many people the wrong way, and I don't mean the public.

7

Of Pranks and Professionals

Colour television arrived when I was still hosting *Frank's Bandstand* in 1966. CBHT inherited a couple of colour cameras from Expo 67, but we didn't get to use them. Neither did *The Don Messer Show*. To turn the Messer show to colour, a couple of film gizmos were attached to the old black and white cameras. The show was shot on colour film, which had to be whisked to Toronto every week for processing by Bill Langstroth (the producer) and Rolf Blei (the technical producer). Bill recalled one trip they made where Rolf was sitting in the window seat of the aircraft. Rolf flew for the Luftwaffe during World War Two, and while looking out the plane's window, he donned a monocle and stuck a cigarette into a long cigarette holder, turned to Bill and said, "It's a lovely day for a raid." Rolf had a sick but wonderful sense of humour.

With black and white television, makeup was applied to your face in layers. It was the consistency of Betty Crocker cake mix, and it invaded your pores like chocolate milk. CBC had a wonderful makeup artist in the person of Jim Micheili. Jim did character makeup in Toronto for some of their biggest dramas. But even though he was a Brit, he missed Nova Scotia and came home. When colour came to Bell Road, the makeup changed from thick to thin and we were quite appreciative of that.

CBC was the only game in town on television from 1954 to 1961. No cable. No competition from other stations. No tablets or cellphones. But who watches TV on a cellphone? You need a magnifying glass. It stayed that way until CJCH TV (now CTV) came along. During the '50s, the chair of the FCC (Federal Communications Commission) in the States said, "We have three channels available and there's nothing on." Today, we have three hundred channels and there's still nothing on!

In 1975 a tour company sponsored a trip to the Bahamas. The idea was to take a bunch of travel agents to the West End, near Freeport, then head off to Nassau, where the tour company would show hotel properties to the agents. A group of media people (including me) had the good fortune to be included in the trip. The CBC had and still has strict rules about that, so I had to get permission. I was told yes, but I wasn't to give the tour company any free publicity. I said I wouldn't and I didn't.

The tour company wanted us there for entertainment only. So off we went. We did indeed provide some entertainment for these travel agents, including the ATV cameraman who stood out on his balcony on Sunday morning wrapped in a sheet and pretending to be the Pope. My colleague Doug Arnold went along for the ride, and I recall one morning he woke me up saying my breakfast was here. Breakfast turned out to be a glass of the local liqueur called Nassau Royale.

While dining one evening at the Nassau Beach Hotel, we noticed an American couple eyeing us. The man finally got up the nerve to approach our table with the greeting, "Are you people Canucks?"

"No," I answered, "that's a Vancouver hockey team."

He said, "No, I mean Canucks, Canadians."

Doug turned to him and said, "Are you a Yankee?"

"Hell no," came the reply. "I'm from Florida!"

"I tell you what," says Doug. "If you don't call me a Canuck, I won't call you a Yankee."

He walked away, chewing his cigar with the cameras around his neck literally spinning. I don't like the term "Canuck" when referring to Canadians. It stems from the mid 1800s, although its derivation isn't certain. It's been used by the United States and other countries during World War Two, and there's even a fictional character named Johnny Canuck. But I don't care. It's demeaning and an insult. If the Vancouver hockey team wants to use it, fill your boots. Just don't call me a Canuck.

One of the travel agents on the flight was a young woman from Saint John, who kept insisting that I meet her friend in Halifax. Not only did I meet her, I ended up getting married to her in 1976. Linda Trenholm was a great person, but she and I had little in common. The one thing about being married to Linda was I got a geography lesson from the great province of New Brunswick. I learned to eat ferns (fiddleheads), seaweed (dulse), and shad. Now shad is a fish that's barely edible. I finally rejected it because it has more bones than any other fish in captivity. I also rejected fiddleheads and dulse, but they are practically staples in New Brunswick and I felt a bit guilty. Linda's father made frequent trips to a place called Pocologan for clams. There are very few

With my partner in bad jokes, Doug Saunders.

things in the shellfish world that rival steamed clams, so I really got into those. That marriage lasted five years.

I was sitting at my desk one day in the late '70s when a producer walked by with a guy I had seen before. His name was Doug Saunders and the chemistry was instant. I saw the gleam in his eyes and said to myself, "I'm gonna work with this guy." Sure enough, it came to pass that the two of us were assigned to the supper-hour show. I did the news. Doug did the sports. Doug had worked at CHNS and CJCH before throwing his lot in with the Corp. He hailed from Northern Ontario, and worked private radio there and in Halifax. That's when radio was radio and not the automated poop that pretends to be radio today.

Doug and I got away with a lot at CBC. We did the news seriously, the weather semi-seriously, and didn't mess with the sports. But after it was all over, we had fun. One night I went into another studio and found a sickly plant that someone had left there to die. I put it between Doug and me and he asked me what it was. I said it was a heavy water plant and it was dying because there was no heavy water. A bit of explanation would be in order here. The province ran a couple of heavy water plants which made "heavy" water for nuclear power plants. Nova Scotia wasn't using nuclear power, so we had to sell it somewhere else, and somewhere else wasn't buying. That's only if you didn't get the joke.

Another night Doug ended the sports and I was missing from the studio. He said, "Frank, where are you?" Cut to Frank on a ladder in the parking lot with a cloth washing the microwave installations. "Sorry, Doug, but it's my turn to do the dishes."

Some typical repartee on *The Maritimes Tonight* might go like this. Frank says, "I hear you had to shoot your dog."

Doug says, "Yeah."

Frank says, "Was he mad?"

Doug says, "Well, he wasn't too happy."

Doug says, "I have a brother in Alaska."

Frank says, "Nome?"

Doug says, "Of course I know him. He's my brother."

Frank says, "I'm going to visit my sister in Pennsylvania."

Doug says, "Erie?"

Frank says, "I wouldn't call her eerie. She's a little weird."

If you missed any of those gems of humour, consider yourself lucky.

We were called into the program director's office from time to time and were given a dressing down for our lack of seriousness. CBC management had no sense of humour. The journalists were running the corporation; many of them had been elevated into management, and most of them couldn't run a two-car funeral. This irreverence gained us the title "credible clowns." The phrase was coined by a professor of language at a media school outside Montreal. He used to play our tapes for these budding journalists in order to keep them honest and gain some sense of humour.

I remember a session in the program director's office where he accused us of talking about breaking wind (or farts, if you will) on the air. On the night in question, Doug was giving results from a World Figure Skating contest, and he was talking about the triple lutz and other figure skating twirls and such. I said at the end of the show that he had done a triple flutterblast in the newsroom earlier that evening. Of course I was talking about farts, but we never thought the PD would ever pick up on it.

The hard facts were these: the audience loved the show, and the crew loved working on it, but management, not so much. During the early '90s, the guy in charge of programming for the CBC came up with what he thought was a brilliant idea. Scrap the late news and put on artsy-fartsy stuff in that time slot. Move *The National* back to nine p.m., put on ballet or some other elitist programming, and turn back the CBC to the '50s.

It lasted a year, and things went back to the way they were.

The idea man was Ivan Fecan. I first met Ivan a few years before he became Mister Television. He was producing a radio show out of Winnipeg and decided to come to Halifax and do a show on the indigenous black people of Nova Scotia. He asked that I be assigned to it, and I found myself in a storefront on Gottingen Street introducing a choir from North Preston.

Ivan and I got along famously, and the next thing I knew he was back in Halifax. He invited me to lunch at the Dresden Arms restaurant on Dresden Row, where he dropped a bit of a bombshell. Apparently, he had been asked to take over the program director's job at CBLT, the CBC's flagship station in Toronto. He wanted my advice on whether or not he should take the job. I said, yes, take it. But get some TV experience. He did more than that. He went to the U.S. and became an observer and kind of intern at NBC. He was probably the best PD ever to darken the doors of the CBC and sooner than later he became a vice president. His one major goof was implementing this elitist plan that sent the CBC back to the Dark Ages. Shortly after that, Ivan found himself at CTV, where he became the head honcho. There's more about Ivan Fecan in Lloyd Robertson's book, *That's The Kind Of Life It's Been*.

Speaking of Lloyd Robertson, I first met him in 1973. He was anchoring *The National*, and I was working out of Halifax. We were both in Charlottetown for the Prince Edward Island centennial celebrations. I was doing some local "stuff" and Lloyd was reporting to the network. He was standing on a pedestal on a sidewalk in downtown Charlottetown. He had a telex (earphone) in one ear that hooked him into the mobile unit a few metres from his position. In the other ear, another telex gave him commands from the central control room in Toronto. The Toronto production assistant said, "Lloyd, you have sixty seconds to sign off." Lloyd's mike was on and he gave a flawless performance for one minute, precisely one minute. Lloyd was a pro. He still is.

Lloyd Robertson had the same problem as all other staff announcers at the CBC, including me. We read the news, but we didn't write it. The staff announcers' contract with the CBC said announcers could write the news. The news guild also claimed jurisdiction and the CBC chose to go with the guild. I was told many times by the CBC training department that I was a good writer, but I couldn't write the news.

That problem came to a head when Lloyd tried to do things on *The National* that weren't in his "jurisdiction." He finally got fed up with the constant hassle and was hired away by CTV. The whole story is in his book.

There was a big hole to fill when Lloyd left the CBC. I made some preliminary inquiries about the job and was advised not to bother because the CBC wanted a face that would be familiar to a national audience. Fair enough. But Knowlton Nash left his management post and hired himself to do *The National*. I remember when I arrived in Halifax in 1959, BUP (British United Press) had an office in the bowels of the old CHNS Broadcast House on Tobin Street. The one-person office was manned by the same Knowlton Nash.

I made the Queen Mother's list in June 1979. I had a lot of time for Queen Elizabeth, the Queen Mother. She was a Scot and since Bonnie Prince Charlie never made it to the throne, it was nice to see that a Scot finally did, even though she was married to King George VI. I admired her for the guts shown by her and her husband for staying in London through World War Two when they could have been moved out of harm's way. When I say I made her list, I mean I was invited to a royal reception at Government House in Halifax when she visited in 1979. I was assigned to a crew covering the Queen Mother's arrival at HMCS Shearwater and her subsequent presenting of the Queen's Colours to Canadian Forces Maritime Command. That rather impressive ceremony took place at the base of Citadel Hill, across from the CBC Radio building.

The CBC crew were among those who attended the reception at Government House. As we sipped our beverages and ate our little finger sandwiches (I found a real finger in mine), the Queen Mother worked the room, trying to speak to as many people in the reception line as she could. When she met the CBC people she kept asking them where they were from and the standard answer was "the CBC."

By the time she got to me, she asked, "How many people work at the CBC?" to which I replied, "About half of them, mum." She laughed and said, "That's so funny!" I learned a valuable lesson about royal protocol that day. While covering the arrival at Shearwater, I said on air that people were shaking hands with the Queen Mother. That, my friends, doesn't happen. The Queen Mother shakes hands with you.

I was heavily involved in the union at CBC during the latter half of my career. I was vice president of our CUPE local in 1989 when the great Dartmouth Police strike happened. Dartmouth City Council would not accept binding arbitration to settle a labour management dispute with the city's police force. Council figured they would get the shaft, just like Dartmouth got after amalgamation. So out went the municipal force while RCMP officers moved in to help the chief and his commissioned officers police the city.

One of the guys carrying a picket sign was Sean Brownlow, whose father was once a mayor of Dartmouth after serving his country as an officer in the Royal Canadian Navy. Sean's brother Pat had been a friend of mine since the '60s, and brother Mike was principal at a junior high school near my house. Brother Tim Brownlow I know, but I'm not as close to Tim as I am with the others. I spent ten days in hospital in 2012. When I returned home, Sean Brownlow and his band the Shamrocks showed up at my house one night and entertained me for two hours with Celtic music. The Shamrocks have been together for almost thirty years, and they are a fine bunch of guys.

During the police strike, I wrote a letter to the mayor of Dartmouth expressing my concern about council not wanting binding arbitration when the rank and file police officers were quite willing to accept it. I copied the police union on the letter and they posted it on their bulletin board. *The Daily News* printed portions of the letter and the shit hit the fan. The CBC apparently has a "blue book" that says journalists and anchors cannot do this, even though you might be (as I was) a citizen and taxpayer in the city. The CBC wanted to suspend me and the union (CUPE) said no. The union was prepared to take the CBC to court on a Charter of Rights challenge. The CBC backed off and reassigned me to the weather, and I wasn't allowed on the news until the police strike was over.

Things have changed at CBC over the years. Somebody coined the phrase "cuts of a thousand deaths" (a play on the Chinese form of torture, death by a thousand cuts) and CBC has certainly experienced enough of those. *Gazette* and all its incarnations is still running in a manner of speaking. But it's not the same. The Corp has been decimated by cuts and it's bleeding. And successive governments have cut it to the bone. The surprising thing is that the CBC can still function.

And now, the corporation will lose that fine institution *Hockey Night in Canada* in 2017. It seems Rogers (not on my top ten list of favourite companies) has literally bought the game of hockey as we know it. The CBC is on a slippery slope and that makes me sad. A friend of mine, Linden MacIntrye, decided to retire because of the way things are at CBC. 657 jobs axed, and most of them behind-the-scenes people. MacIntyre thinks these young people should be invested in, not cut. He's right. He left in part to put a familiar face in the public's eye.

The concentration these days seems to be on the News Network and some of the network's anchors on the national program are being given bad advice. They are increasingly talking with their hands and waving their arms in the air in some frenzied way to look natural.

I first noticed it with Carole MacNeil, who's from Antigonish and worked in Fredericton when I was in Halifax. Carole somehow learned to talk with her hands. The people fronting for the entertainment department all do it. In some cases it's a nervous thing. The movie reviewer looks as if he is sending some kind of metaphoric message, or he's a helicopter getting ready for takeoff. As he waves his hands frantically, it takes away most of his credibility. The audience is totally distracted from what the person is saying by the movement of their arms. That's not to say they should sit there like a lump, but there must be another way to present the story. When I was at the CBC, there was such a thing as vocal coaches, but no one was trying to emote by using their hands or arms. I think it's a European thing. Another favourite of mine is resting your chin on your hand while listening to an answer during an interview. That's both pretentious and phony.

In my day, there was also an emphasis on voice. As Don Tremaine said, "You had to have a good set of pipes." I remember a couple of senior announcers from Toronto coming to Halifax one day to show us how to get the proper pitch in your voice. You sit down and put your head between your legs (I'm not making this up), and as you slowly move your upper body back into the sitting position, you say things like, "This is the CBC Radio Network." Your voice should theoretically get deeper as your body rises.

I won't mention names here to avoid embarrassment, but one of our new announcers was going to read the news with me at one p.m. one day, and I suggested that I would do the headlines and he would do the first story. When I finished the headlines, he cupped his hand behind his ear and did the opening piece. I thought it was hilarious. I was about to thank him for the great impression of Gary Owens (the announcer on the U.S. comedy *Laugh-In*) when I realized the guy was being deadly serious. He said singers do it to get the proper pitch in their voice. Lesson learned. The announcer in question was a singer and a hell of a good piano player.

The current Halifax supper-hour show doesn't suffer from arm-waving. It has a more serious problem: it's devoid of personality. The cast are all nice people, but it just doesn't work.

When three people are talking on air, they should try to look at each other when they talk. Sticking your face in the camera when you're talking to someone sitting or standing beside you does not make great television. If you've just witnessed a story that's even mildly amusing, you must have the creativity to make some remark other than "That was funny." There's nothing like stating the obvious.

I have to say, though, that I love the CBC, warts and all. Two of their reporters have defected to CTV recently, but it's no loss. Neither was Brian Williams, who left CBC years ago because he loved spreading his knowledge about anything and CTV had just picked up the rights to the Olympics. He was the Olympics "expert," so he jumped to CTV in order to annoy their audience. No loss for CBC. The biggest loss for the Corp was Lloyd Robertson.

During my time in television I was able to contribute to CBC Radio. I hosted an afternoon radio show with my friend George Jordan. It's still on the air today. *Mainstreet* was and is a mixture of news, music, and current affairs. Every Friday afternoon George and I would come up with a feature we called the Anti-Entertainment Report, an irreverent look at the week's news.

When Queen Elizabeth visited New Brunswick, then premier Richard Hatfield left his overnight bag on the Queen's plane. The bag allegedly contained some pot that Richard liked to inhale now and then. George (who did an amazing impression of Her Majesty) and I did a skit which had Hatfield talking to the Queen about the missing bag. The conversation involved Richard telling her not to worry about the bag. It was a cheap bag. Hatfield called it a "dime" bag.

ACTRA, the performers' union, complained about us doing this feature (because ACTRA members could write copy but CUPE members couldn't), but the CBC stood up for us. We were staff announcers and we could do anything we wanted to do on the program. CBC was good about encouraging staff announcers to use our brains, to come up with new ideas for current shows. Radio producers were key; they'd go to management and ask for a specific announcer or personality.

George Jordan was and is still my friend. He came to CBC after a stint in private radio and some acting jobs he managed to get while bumming around California. After doing the radio show (and some television) for a few years, he left the CBC, ran for politics, and started his own consulting firm. He has recently bought into those information radio stations around the Maritimes and has done some work for Seaside FM. Dinners at the Jordans' were memorable. I remember George and me killing an entire bottle of brandy and he launched into his evangelist impression. He kept his dinner guests in stitches.

I also hosted a national radio show called *Country Roads* with a very talented musician, Vic Mullen. The producer was Ira Stewart and we recorded the show once a week in the old studio H on Argyle Street.

I can't remember the exact year, but Ira, Vic, and I flew to Nashville to record some bluegrass groups. We were accompanied by Glenn Meisner, a great technician who later became a great radio producer. We spent three days in Music City and recorded tracks at the Johnny Cash studio. Those were the days when the CBC had money.

8

England, Trudeau, and Politics (Sort Of)

I went to England in 1981 with my companion at the time, Elizabeth Stevens. Liz was the big communications honcho at St. Mary's. It really pissed her off when people referred to the university as SMU. She has a wonderful daughter named Caitlin who accompanied us on the trip. Caitlin now lives in New Brunswick and has a couple of kids herself. She's one of the few people who can get away with calling me "Frankie."

We went to London and didn't see the Queen, but I saw the Changing of the Guard at Buckingham Palace. Early one morning I jumped on a double-decker bus and asked the conductor (they still had them back then) to alert me when we neared the Palace. He seemed a bit standoffish as he sat on a seat near me. He looked at me and said, "You a Yank, are ya?"

"No," I said.

"Irish then?"

"Nope." I let him stew for a few seconds before I blurted out that I was Canadian.

When I said that, he opened up like a sieve. He said he loved Canadians and he had been to Vancouver, of all places. He gave me a running commentary on everything I should be seeing in London, and said a fond farewell when we got to the Palace.

The next morning I was off to the BBC, or Beeb, as it's fondly known in Britain. I was shown around by one of their guides in a prearranged tour. I saw the studio where a German bomb had entered the building and lodged itself in the ceiling of one of the radio studios. The announcer (who used to wear tuxedos) didn't miss a word. The bomb was a dud. (Similarly, in October 1940, when the first bomb to hit the BBC exploded and killed seven, announcer Bruce Belfrage calmly continued reading the news.)

I was ushered into a radio studio in BBC 2, where a couple of news presenters were about to do a half-hour news program. Their Moscow correspondent was on the line, and they told him Canada was in the studio. His reply was, "The whole damn country?" I love the British sense of humour. *Monty Python's Flying Circus* is one of my favourite TV programs of all time. They were fifteen minutes to air when one of the guys asked me if I wanted a drink. I said, "Sure, I could use a glass of water." "Water, old chap, who said anything about water?" So I had some vodka and orange juice. Gad! The British are so civilized.

Liz and I travelled from London to Leeds on the train, and Bill, the husband of Liz's friend Sheila, picked us up at the station. Bill and Sheila Rusby lived in Ilkley, not far from Leeds in Yorkshire. We spent New Year's Eve in a three-hundred-year-old pub and dined on pheasant. There are hundreds of pheasant farms in

England, and we ate in style. I kept hitting my head when I went from room to room. Seems when the pub was built people were shorter than they are today.

Bill and I spent a pleasant Sunday afternoon in a pub out on the moors. The landlord was a great host and when you looked outside, you might have expected Robin Hood and his Merry Men to come riding down the narrow road. There was a professor there from a local university who asked me how it felt to live in the colonies. I knew he was kidding so I shrugged it off. He then wanted to know about this fellow Trudeau (our PM at the time). He loved Pierre and told me that most of the academics in Britain felt Pierre was quite the guy.

Here's my Trudeau story. My father's sister Eileen lived in Antigonish most of her adult life and was a fixture in the community. She married Eric Henry, whose grandfather was not only mayor of Halifax, but one of the Fathers of Confederation. William Alexander Henry lived for a time on Barrington Street. His house has been designated a heritage property. My aunt Eileen was a real character. She served publicly in many ways, including as the first woman elected to Antigonish town council and as deputy mayor. Like my father, she highly valued language and was indefatigable in her fight for a local library. She wrote a column, "Around Town and County," for the Antigonish newspaper *The Casket* as well as writing and publishing books of poetry.

In *Comfort Me With Apples*, she pays tribute to her son Courtney, who died from a self-inflicted gunshot wound. As she mourned Courtney's loss, she turned to me for comfort and I was happy to provide it since I was now the senior male in the Cameron family. She asked if I would be her escort in Ottawa as she received the Order of Canada. I agreed, and we were off to the capital city.

We arrived at Government House, and I went downstairs to don the tuxedo I had rented for the occasion. That's where I met Bruce Cockburn. The singer-songwriter was about to receive his Order of Canada and we struck up a great conversation, particularly when he found out I worked at the CBC. There was something about Bruce that I can't quite put my finger on. He sings about a tree falling in the forest and nobody cares, and other angry songs such as "If I Had a Rocket Launcher." He is an environmental and political activist, but in my conversation with him I didn't get the impression that he was ready to march.

With Aunt Eileen in tow, we went to the ceremony and then to the Great Hall where Pierre Trudeau was holding court. Say what you will about Pierre, he had a way with women. My aunt swooned in his presence and I had to apologize for working for the CBC. Mr. Trudeau thought I might be hiding a microphone or a camera. It re-enforced my opinion of him, which was always a good one.

I got to know Ottawa pretty well during my time at the CBC because of various trips for union business. I sat on a union management committee, which was given the task of doing something with the "staff" announcers. Most of us were wrongly given titles like "mouths with feet" and referred to by that phrase I mentioned earlier, "golden-throated relics of a bygone era." I wasn't insulted by any of this, knowing from whence it came – the journalists who usurped our jurisdiction in writing the news, and the CBC caved into them. That committee contained many "mouths with feet," including George McLean of *The National*. Most of the management on the committee were nice people, but they were charged with trying to ease the staff announcer out of the news department and into the booth, which was basically the hinterland. Those who delivered the news were now journalists or broadcasters, not staff announcers. But some very talented people were staff announcers.

One lovely day I was coming out of a hotel in Ottawa and I heard a loud car horn. In the car was my old pal, Mike Duffy. He had recently jumped to CTV, and proceeded to tell me the story of how he made the last plane out of South Vietnam when the North Vietnamese took over.

He also told me that his job at CTV was great, but he really wanted to be a senator. I told him he was full of it, but he insisted, and eventually he became a senator. Mike knows people all across the country and has done a lot in broadcasting. We've recently been in touch by e-mail. Mike Duffy's story is far from over.

When my children were small, we had a babysitter who lived across the street. Like Linda Trenholm, Chris Lewell had a New Brunswick connection. Her dad was born and raised in Saint John. I first met Chris in the late '60s when she was babysitting Seanna and Mark. We lost track of each other for a few years. She was married twice, as was I, and we again met up in the mid '80s. One thing led to another, and in 1987 we married (each other). Chris has become my rock through my retirement from CBC, going back to CHNS, and finally ending up at Seaside FM. But, even more important, she has been with me through my medical ordeal in the past couple of years. She lost her mother years ago to Alzheimer's disease and her father died in 2013. Chris was very close to both her parents, and I loved them both too.

When I married Chris I was an instant stepdad. Her daughter Tracy became part of my life, and I loved her from the get-go. Tracy presented us with a granddaughter named Kayleigh in 2000 and another granddaughter named Zoie in 2011. Grandchildren just add more and more joy to our lives.

While I'm at it, my oldest granddaughter Rebecca is now living just a few blocks away from her grandfather. Rebecca has a brother and three sisters living in beautiful British Columbia. And yes, they're all my grandchildren. If my daughter Seanna is anything, she's productive. And I now have a great-granddaughter. When Seanna called me to tell me the news, she said, "Dad, you're a great-grandfather!"

"I know that," I replied.

"No, Dad, you have a great-granddaughter!"

"I have a number of great granddaughters!" I said. "Which one are you talking about?"

Fortunately, Seanna inherited my sick sense of humour. Otherwise, we could have kept the Abbott and Costello routine going for days.

I had a go at politics in 1997. I ran for the Liberal party in Dartmouth North. I came a respectable third behind the NDP and the Progressive Conservatives. It was quite an experience. It gave me new insights into political parties. I happened to be running for the Liberals, but they're all the same. The leader is a figurehead. The party is actually run by the "old boys' club" operating out of the back rooms. There are those who will show up at your headquarters saying if they vote for you, they need new teeth or their van needs to be upgraded. This is pure blackmail, but it's part of our political system. Years ago a pint of rum bought you a vote (maybe) and after the election, who's to say they voted for you in the first place.

I allowed a reporter columnist for the now defunct *Daily News* to follow me while I was campaigning in Dartmouth, and he wrote a very damaging article inferring that I was a racist, and that I would only be a "part-time" politician. There was a black man who wanted me to step aside so he could run, and the riding committee said no. End of story. This reporter asked me if I was going to work when the Nova Scotia Legislature wasn't sitting. I said yes. CHNS (to their credit) gave me the time off (with pay) to run. And when I wasn't sitting in the House I would be working, just as Gerry Lawrence did when he was sitting in the House.

Frankly, I should have known better. This guy was out to get me, and he did. He helped to ruin what could have been a budding political career. On the other hand, maybe he did me a favour. I wasn't crazy about the backroom stuff anyway, and as I said, the parties are all the same. I hope this guy is enjoying his career with Sun media, where they never let the facts get in the way of a good story.

9

In Which I Rub Elbows With Some Famous People

I'm going to do some name-dropping now. Anne Murray was a member of *Singalong Jubilee* when we met. She released her first recording in 1968 on Arc Records. The title song was "What About Me" and Arc did well from that album. It's no longer available, but I have it on vinyl and CD. She had made the big time when Capitol Records released her second album in 1969, *This Way Is My Way*, and Capitol decided to do a single (45) from it, with "Thirsty Boots" as the A side and "Hard As I Try" on the B side. "Thirsty Boots" was first recorded by Judy Collins in 1966. I was appalled. This album contained a perfectly good – no, a great – song, "Snowbird," written by P.E.I.'s Gene MacLellan. I immediately called the A&R guy for Capitol Canada, Paul White (I wasn't the only one), and said, "What the hell were you thinking?"

"Thirsty Boots" was toast and "Snowbird" became a number one hit. Anne recorded several of Gene's songs

With Anne Murray in 1978 when she received an honorary degree from Saint Mary's University.

on subsequent albums. The CBC did *Sounds 68*, a half-hour show on Saturday nights. I hosted it and Anne was featured on two of those shows. She also spent a season on *Frank's Bandstand*. It was during that season I realized Anne has a wicked sense of humour. Her book *All of Me* is an honest look at her life and she tells it like it was. I highly recommend it. I know Anne Murray but there are things in this book, sometimes intimate things, that I never knew. I love her, and after reading her book, I love her even more. When the Anne Murray Centre opened in Springhill in 1989, I covered the opening for CBC Radio.

Her manager for many years was a guy named Leonard Rambeau. He was a victim of colon cancer, a cause that Anne fervently supports. I met Leonard when he was a student at St. Mary's University and was Anne's biggest fan. He became her manager after graduation and was with her through thick and thin. She pays a great tribute to Leonard in her book. Anne is now retired. She told me she loves retirement, and she "got out" in her prime and doesn't regret it.

Another mutual friend is Georges Hebert, who made regular appearances on *Frank's Bandstand* starting in 1964. Georges was with the Brunswick Playboys, a group from Moncton. They did a song called "Too Blind To See," which became a local hit on CHNS and is featured on *Do You Want to Dance – The Best of Frank's Bandstand* LP, an album regrettably no longer available. Georges Hebert went on to become Anne Murray's principal guitarist and toured with her for many years. He's still in the business and produces many artists, including my friend Blain Henshaw, from his studio in Bedford.

Blain and I go way back. He was a mouthpiece for many politicians for a lot of years in the provincial government. He was a "civil" servant, so he didn't serve at the whim of any political party. Upon retirement he returned to his first love, singing and songwriting, and he also volunteers at Seaside FM, giving him a chance to put his vast radio experience to good use. We've been great friends for many years.

I met the California group the Four Preps in 1965 when they visited Halifax for a show at St. Mary's University. They'd all been Hollywood High students together when they formed the quartet in 1956. They came to CHNS for an interview, one that was kind of cheeky for those days. The thing I liked about these guys was their impressions of other groups such as the Platters and Dion and the Belmonts. The lead singer, Bruce Belland, had some fun with me during the interview. When he said something that might have been slightly off-colour, I told him if he kept it up I was going to get my pink slip (fired). "Gee," he said, "you wear a pink slip? Mine are blue."

If the interview happened today, the politically correct police would be all over that remark like a wet blanket. During that era, it was okay to be somewhat politically incorrect, and the Preps pushed the envelope with risqué lyrics to songs such as "Princess Poopooly Has Plenty Papaya" and "She was only the Dean of Men's Daughter." These gems and others can be found on their Capitol Records album *Campus Confidential* recorded live at their UCLA concert.

The Four Preps' biggest hit was "26 Miles," a salute to the island of Catalina off the coast of California. The verse I like in that song goes, "Forty kilometres in a leaky old boat, anything that'll stay afloat." They pronounce the word kilometre correctly (KILL-im-eeter).

The British affectation of the word is kill-AW-mutter, which is used by most people in North America. It's wrong. Do we say mill-IM-mutter? No. It's MILL-im-eeter. These are French words that have been anglicized by the British and the Americans.

Neil Diamond came to town in 1966. I met him, but that's as far as it went. He had a small number of hits then. "Cherry Cherry" and "Solitary Man" come to mind. But Neil composed in the Brill building in New York during the mid '60s where he wrote hundreds of songs. Some he recorded. Some were done by others. He penned "I'm a Believer" and "A Little Bit Me, A Little Bit You," made famous by the Monkees, and Jay and the Americans' hit "Sunday and Me." He sang most of those songs at St. Mary's that night. Other stars who got their start in the Brill building include Carole King and her ex-husband Gerry Goffin, Neil Sedaka, Hal David, Burt Bacharach, Tommy Boyce, Bobby Hart, Sonny Bono, and even Canada's Andy Kim. I won't list all the residents here, but it's longer than both my arms.

Gene Pitney was, is, and forever shall be one of my favourite singer-songwriters. He managed, in an era of British-dominated music, to do well on both sides of the Atlantic. Born in Hartford, Connecticut, in 1940, he was also part of the Brill building entourage, where he wrote songs for other artists, including "Hello, Mary Lou" recorded by Rick Nelson and "Rubber Ball" by Bobby Vee. He scored a hit with one of the Phil Spector groups, the Crystals. "He's a Rebel" went to the top of the charts in 1962. (It was actually Darlene Love of the Blossoms who sang the song. Phil Spector credited it to the Crystals, who were touring with Pitney at the time. Darlene Love also sang with Bob B. Soxx and the Blue Jeans. You can hear Darlene and other backup singers recount their experiences in the documentary *20 Feet From Stardom*.)

The song in number two spot? Gene's "Only Love Can Break a Heart," a Burt Bacharach-Hal David composition. That same year, Gene recorded "The Man Who Shot Liberty Valance," another Bacharach-David offering, which reached number four spot on the Billboard chart. In 1963, he came to Halifax and spent a week doing shows at the old Armview Theatre. I had the pleasure of introducing him, and he sang "I Wanna Love My Life Away," "Every Breath I Take," and many more. I found Gene to be a solid guy, a consummate musician, and a very funny individual, even though he was painfully shy. I used to hear from him now and then, even after I joined the CBC. Unlike Bobby Curtola, Gene and I eventually lost touch. Gene Pitney died of natural causes while touring Britain in 2006.

I mentioned Burton Cummings when I was explaining *Music Hop* (*Frank's Bandstand*) and the fact that the *Music Hop* show from Winnipeg featured the Guess Who with Burton Cummings and Randy Bachman. I actually didn't meet Burton until the late '90s when he came to town with his one-man show *Up Close and Alone*. He was somewhat standoffish, but I managed a brief conversation with him. He spent about ninety minutes at the Rebecca Cohn auditorium and did a wicked impression of Gordon Lightfoot singing a Rod Stewart song.

I first met Gordon Lightfoot in the mid '60s. It was back in the coffee house days, and he was appearing at an old coffee house on Sackville Street. I was given the task (more like an honour) of introducing him. Before the show, his guitarist, Red Shea, took me aside and asked if I would introduce a special song that Lightfoot wrote about the railroad in Canada. The CBC had commissioned Gordon to write the song and he was trying it out on audiences around the country. He sang the "Canadian Railroad Trilogy" for seven or eight minutes.

Dead silence for five seconds. Then, a standing ovation that lasted for five minutes. The audience loved it, and there were few dry eyes in the house. Lightfoot was, and still is, Canada's poet laureate. In 1968 he played to a sold-out audience at the old Capitol Theatre, and in 1970 he came back to appear at the opening of the Halifax Metro Centre.

The Capitol Theatre, a Halifax landmark on Barrington Street near the foot of Spring Garden Road destroyed in the days of development at all costs, was host to big shows and movies. It had loges and a balcony and it could seat about a thousand people. Loges are halfway between the downstairs and the balcony of a theatre. I emceed a lot of stuff there, including the Clancy Brothers and Tommy Makem. I even wore one of those white wool sweaters that were common for Irish performers back then for some reason. I found these guys were hilarious. The more Irish whiskey they consumed, the better they sounded. I spent only a few hours with them, but I was impressed. On the serious side, "The Patriot Game" is one of their best songs. And for fun, "They're Removing Father's Grave to Build a Sewer."

Another show at the old Capitol Theatre was sponsored by Eaton's. I had a good friend who for many years was advertising manager for Eaton's in Halifax. Gary MacPherson was a New Glasgow boy who could sell anything to anybody. Eaton's used to buy advertising time on CHNS, and I remember many nights Gary would arrive at the station about 6:45 p.m. with a new product he wanted me to talk about on the department store's commercial at 7:15. The commercials put my ad lib skills to the test.

So it was on a Saturday afternoon in the mid '60s I donned a loincloth, did my best Tarzan impression, and co-hosted a fashion show with Carole Taylor, who was working for Eatons and the CTV network. Carole was working out of Toronto at the time, but she ended up in Vancouver, where she sat on city council and was elected as a Liberal in the British Columbia government. She became the minister of finance, married the mayor of Vancouver, Art Phillips, sat on the CBC Board of Governors, and is currently the chancellor of Simon Fraser University. Not too shabby.

Gary died in 2012 and I miss his perpetual smile and upbeat personality.

While I was finishing a shift in TV one day in the mid '80s, one of our music producers asked if I could give a young woman a lift home. I was to wait for her and return her to the main studio on Bell Road. Her band was recording in the studio and she had to run home to make a quick clothing change. A seventeen-year-old student at Queen Elizabeth High School, she was lead singer in the band known as the October Game. Her name was (and still is) Sarah McLauchlan. Sarah was raised in Halifax, but after a year at the College of Art, she promptly moved to Vancouver, where she signed a record deal, and the rest, as they say, is history. She was a year into her recording career when I had the chance to interview her on CBC radio, and I remember the radio producer was getting a kick out of her talking to a friend while waiting to go on the air. We had a great chat by phone from her home in Vancouver. I can say, I knew her when. I know millions of people around the world feel the same way about her, but Sarah holds a special place in my heart.

10

Retirement, Scotland, and Seaside

After the death of my mother in 1993, I began to think seriously of retirement from the CBC. It happened a year later. I had the formula to retire (age plus years of service had to total eighty-five) and I said goodbye to the Corporation in 1995. Doug Saunders and I retired on the same day. Two days later, we were hosting the morning show on my old alma mater, CHNS. There were three of us on the program – Doug, me, and a wonderful woman named M.J. (Martha Jo) Finnamore. There were rumours at the time that I was having some sort of illicit affair with M.J. That was not true.

We had a great time on the morning show, but CHNS was not the same as it was in the '60s. Back then, while I was working in Halifax, a guy named Merv Russell was doing the DJ thing in Saint John, New Brunswick. Merv paid his dues and came to Halifax after starting a radio station in Sussex, New Brunswick. McLean Hunter bought the station from *The Chronicle Herald* and Merv became manager. He was still manager in 1995 when Doug and I joined the company, then owned by Robert Pace and part of the Maritime Broadcasting System.

Doug was the first to leave CHNS, and I stayed on with M.J. for a time before she also left the station. M.J. now lives in Fredericton, New Brunswick, where she's host of *In Tune* at CJRI on the Faithway Radio Network and does commercials for Seaside FM. Doug eventually moved to Glace Bay where he hosts the morning show at The Coast. Doug and I had a falling out mostly because of a misunderstanding. I don't get to Cape Breton and he doesn't get here, so we're kind of in limbo.

Unfortunately, CHNS, like most radio stations in Canada, had become automated and it just wasn't the same. We had a program director who was too young to run an oldies station, with eight hundred songs which we played over and over and over again. When I challenged him to play some different songs, he said, "They didn't test well." I was told the station had brought in some people who were oldies fans. The station played some songs for them and these people literally picked most of the songs that CHNS played ad nauseum. That sounds so American. Obviously, it didn't work. So when I was told a song didn't test well, I'd roll my eyes and shake my head.

I'd forgotten more about '60s music than he would ever know. There were lots of bean counters in the station then, and we had two guys who worked for the company who lived in Moncton and Charlottetown respectively. They would drop into the station once a week to attend our morning meeting. I recall one morning one of them asked me why I played "Love Me Warm and Tender" by Paul Anka. He said he had never heard the song, that it was never a hit, and why did I stray from the playlist of eight hundred songs? I quickly informed him that indeed "Love Me Warm and Tender" was one of Paul Anka's biggest hits, that the fact he had never heard the song meant nothing to me, and that the playlist was not long enough. I had age on my side on that one, but the playlist was not extended and it was these guys who helped run CHNS into the ground.

Merv tried his best, but more often than not, he was usurped. We made some attempts to "buy the book," as Merv called it. Every station does it except CBC radio. You jam all the contests you can think of while BBM (Bureau of Broadcast Measurement) were taking ratings – things such as trips to the sunny south or cash jackpots worth up to fifty thousand dollars. It's an old game. CHNS did it back in the '60s. CHNS was the first radio station in Halifax in 1926, and it was the first to switch to FM in the early part of this century.

I blame radio station owners and managers for the sorry state of private radio today. They are listening to endless consultants – mostly American – who don't know their ass from a hole in the ground. These so-called experts are either failed on-air personalities or clever fast talkers who can pull the wool over most sets of eyes.

Stations are staffed by young people who aren't allowed to exhibit their personality (provided they have one) and they are nothing more than robots. Managers of these stations are tasked with making money for the owners, and most owners nowadays are big corporations who don't give a hoot for the audience. Their mantra is "Show me the money!" If you check the BBM ratings, you will consistently find CBC Radio is number one in most markets and the rest of them fall in behind. They're all going for the bubble-gummers (a '60s expression meaning teenagers or pre-teens).

The private stations provide no alternative to the dance, hip hop, and other music that exploits our young people. It's their grandparents, even great-grandparents, who like real rock and roll and pop music from the 1950s, '60s and even the '70s.

Satellite radio had reared its head in the '90s and the over-the-air stations were shaking in their boots. Why? Because the commercial stations had nowhere to go. If they had paused taken a deep breath, and listened to their audience for once, they would have realized that satellite radio is just Muzak with feet. It provides satellite national and international sports programming and even the CBC has a couple of channels, but satellite radio can't deliver local news, and besides, it hasn't been technically perfected yet, so you can lose it in certain terrain.

I couldn't hang on at CHNS any longer. Lucky for me, though, the radio gods are a persistent bunch. I was coming out of a pharmacy one day and this guy practically accosted me. His name is Wayne Harrett and we have since become good friends. He asked if I would be interested in doing a radio show for the then 50-watt station Seaside Radio. CFEP has amassed a huge audience, even though the signal is spotty. But we have permission to go on the CBC tower, and the stronger, more reliable signal will increase our audience. The station is manned by volunteers, many of whom are retired broadcasters like me.

Community stations have sprung up all over this country, mainly because the radio listener has become more focused. It's a bit complicated, but many people are tired of music that's too loud and features bad poetry and a drum machine. Seaside FM works on a very simple premise. The station listens to the audience and they listen to us. We have the best audience in the world. They range from baby boomers to people in their eighties, and they want to hear familiar music that resonates with them. Being at Seaside is just like the old days, when the radio announcer had more control and listeners enjoyed the DJ's personality. We even have turntables.

As so often happens in life, when one thing is going well, something else doesn't. After a good run of being healthy, in 2012 I was diagnosed with an advanced case of bladder cancer. My bladder was removed in October of that year and I now have an ostomy. I have a great support system and I just take things one day at a time.

One of the reasons I retired was to travel a bit. I went to Britain in 2013 with a group of our listeners. The deal was that if we could deliver thirty-five people to the tour company in England, we could have a coach all to ourselves. We could only manage twenty-five, so we were joined by ten Australians and a couple of Americans. Before the trip, I liked Australians. Now, I love them. And the couple from Los Angeles were a credit to their country. When one of our number choked on food while dining in Scotland, Michael (the American) performed the Heimlich maneuver and literally saved her life. We named him Sir Michael after that.

As the coach headed north toward Scotland, I was taking in the countryside of England, with its fields of sheep and old airfields used during World War Two. We saw remnants of the old control towers where young men and women guided the Spitfires or Hawker Hurricanes into the sky to take on the Luftwaffe during the Battle of Britain. Many of the pilots (average age nineteen) came from Canada and you could almost see aircraft taking off from these old bases, which were long ago turned back to the sheep farmers.

While en route I noticed that the road signs in Britain have reverted to miles instead of kilometres, and there's no such thing as a kilogram of meat. In Scotland the road signs are in English and Gaelic, no doubt a gesture to assure the Scots that England still cares, and that the Scottish independence movement gets nowhere. On the way to Edinburgh I met the nicest Scottish separatists you'd ever want to encounter. They asked where we were from and as soon as Canada was mentioned, they wanted to talk about Quebec. As Sheldon on the *Big Bang Theory* would say, "Bazinga!"

We arrived in Edinburgh, Scotland, and for some reason I felt as if I were home. Our hotel was next door to the zoo, so we had to visit. It was clean and well kept, but we couldn't see the Chinese panda bears because one of them was pregnant. I'm not sure, but I think it was the female. Since we couldn't see the pandas we did the next best thing. We ate at a Chinese restaurant across the street from the hotel. We did manage to see the koalas. That's where my Australian friends came in. We were calling them koala bears. They're not bears. They're not even members of the bear family. Lesson learned.

Edinburgh Castle, built on an extinct volcano, looms large over the city from its hilltop above the Firth of Forth. The Scottish National War Memorial is housed in the castle itself, and there is a room with books of names of the war dead of the two world wars. The online Scottish war memorial site says, "The north side of the Hall of Honour is divided by columns into bays, each dedicated to a different regiment and decorated with colours and battle honours ... On the broad shelf in front of each of the bays, the names of the dead are listed in leather-bound books."

You aren't allowed to take pictures, but visitors are invited to look through the books for their own war dead. It was there I found the name of Augustus Frank Cameron, my grandfather. I mentioned in an earlier chapter that he was killed in World War One. These books contain the names of Scots. It didn't matter where you lived. After all these years of hearing about my grandfather and how he died, to be standing there in the country of our ancestors, looking at his name – my name – and see recorded there when and where he died, I felt not just closure but a sense of peace. It was a pretty amazing moment.

Then there was the stop in Culloden. The Battle of Culloden took place in 1746 and was the last hurrah for Bonnie Prince Charlie. He and the Jacobites, Scottish clans buoyed by some French and Irish mercenaries and a few disgruntled English soldiers, took on a superior English force at Culloden, near Inverness in the Scottish Highlands. Charles Edward Stuart managed to escape, but the rest of his forces were cut to pieces, thus ending the Jacobite rebellion.

As the bus pulled into the parking lot beside Culloden, I felt the hair stand up on the back of my neck. I was engulfed by a strange feeling. I felt I had been here before. But I wasn't. I could almost hear my ancestors calling me. Alexander Cameron would have been too young to have fought in the Battle of Culloden. But I'm glad he chose to come to Canada in 1773. Otherwise, I would not have been able to write this book. Hell, I wouldn't even be here. I said at the beginning that this would take a while. But I can now say I saw from whence I came.